SOME ASPECTS OF BARI HISTORY

SOME ASPECTS OF BARI HISTORY

A Comparative Linguistic and Oral Tradition Reconstruction

Bureng G.V. Nyombe

University of Nairobi Press

First published 2007 by
University of Nairobi Press (UONP)
Jomo Kenyatta Memorial Library
University of Nairobi
P.O. Box 30197 – 00100 Nairobi
E-mail: nup@uonbi.ac.ke
www.uonbi.ac.ke/press

The University of Nairobi Press supports and promotes University of Nairobi's objectives of discovery, dissemination and preservation of knowledge and stimulation of intellectual and cultural life by publishing works of the highest quality in association with partners in different parts of the world. In doing so, it adheres to the University's tradition of excellence, innovation and scholarship.

© George Bureng V. Nyombe 2007.

All rights reserved. Except for the quotation of fully acknowledged short passages for the purposes of criticism, review, research or teaching, no part of this publication may be reproduced, stored in any retrieval system, or transmitted in any form or means without a prior written permission from the University of Nairobi Press.

University of Nairobi Library Cataloging-in Publication Data
    Nyombe, Bureng G.V. Some Aspects of Bari History: A
    Comparative Linguistic and Oral Tradition Reconstruction/ by
    B.G.V.
    Nyombe. – Nairobi: University of Nairobi Press 2007, pp. 182
    1. Bari Languange
    I. Title
    PL 806 N9

ISBN 9966 846 97 2

Printed by
Starbright Services Ltd
P.O. Box 66949-00200
Nairobi

Contents

List of Tables, Figures and Diagrams ix

Foreword xi

Acknowledgements xv

Introduction   1

1. The Bari: Geographical Distribution   5
    Socio-economic organization 5
    Pastoral life...7
    Agriculture 11
    Ownership of gardens and allocation of produce 12

2. Language Family   15
    Genetic classification 19
    Typological classification..19
    Areal classification 20
    Diffusion and migration 20

3. Language and Race   23
    Formation of the plural from the singular 28
    Formation of the singular from the plural 29
    The article...29
    Numerals 30
    The copula 31
    Hamites: myth or reality 34
    Current status of Nilotic languages 37

4. Bari in Pre-History — 39
Migration vs diffusion 44
Migration of Nilotes 47

5. Bari Migration — 51
Migration from the East 53
The Bari migrated from the North 55
The Bari-speakers: myth or reality 61
Cultural difference 69

6. The Bari Before the Invasion (1500–1840) — 71
Early settlement 71
'Yo'yok (about 1565–1585) 74
The expulsion of the Pari from Liria 75
Lomijikotet (about 1585–1605) 76
Lokoro (about 1605–1625) 77
Kuwuba (about 1625–1645) 77
Pintong (about 1645–1665) 77
Pitnong and Lokuryeje 77
Tombe Lokureje (about 1665–1685): The golden age in Bariland 80
Mödi Lokuryeje (about 1685–1705) 81
Tome Mödi (1705–1725) 82
Mödi (1725–1745) 82
The split of Sindiru (c.1745–1815) 82
Split of Sindiru and the Bilinyang rain dynasty (1765–1785): Subek-lo-Jada 83
Sindiru about 1500 (*an illustration*) 85
Jangara (1785–1815) 85
Pitya-lo-Jangara (1815–1845) 86
The decline of Sindiru (1845–1885) 88
Arabs in Sindiru (1885–1889) 90
Wani (1885–1897) 91

7.	***Bilinyang and Gondokoro (1765–1932)***	***93***
	First contact with outside world	95
	The first European	95
	Subek (1850)	100
	Lako (about 1870)	101
8.	***The Coming of the Foreigners (1839–1883)***	***103***
	Civil war at Gondokoro	108
9.	***Trader-Chiefs (1859–1885)***	***113***
	Samuel Baker (1869–1876)	116
	General Gordon (1877–1880)	120
	Emin Pasha (1881–1887)	123
	The Lado Enclave (1897–1907)	125
	Balkanization of the Bari: (1898–1906)	127
	Wars of succession	129
	Government chiefs	131
10.	***Socio-Political Change***	***133***
	Christianity and Islam in Bariland	133
	Socio-political change	139
	Socio-economic change	143

End Notes	***145***
Bibliography	***153***
Glossary of unfamiliar words	***159***
Index	***163***

List of Tables, Figures and Diagrams

Tables

Table 1: *Food crops grown in Bari* 12
Table 2: *System of naming calendar months in Bari* 14
Table 3: *Bari and Nubian verbal roots* 26
Table 4: *Roots common to Nubian and Bari* 32

Figures

Figure 1: *Geographical location of the Bari-speaking peoples and possible route of migration.* 59
Figure 2: *An illustration of Bari activities* 64
Figure 3: *Old grained stone with rainstones at Grave of Sada* 85
Figure 4: *Rainstones* 85
Figure 5: *Shindirru rainshrine (The Bari)* 85
Figure 6: *An illustration of Bari homestead* 106
Figure 7: *View Northwards from Juba, Jebel Lado in the distance (The Bari)* 136
Figure 8: *Sketch Map of the Central District: Mongolla Province* 141

Diagrams

Diagram 1: *Proto-Nilotic dialects* 42
Diagram 2: *Three genetic classification methods* 43
Diagram 3: *Two primary genetic groups* 49

Foreword

Some Aspects of Bari History: A Comparative Linguistic and Oral History Reconstruction is about a history of a people known as the Bari. The Bari people are found in the Sudan but other related Bari groupings are found across the boarder in Uganda and the Democratic Republic of the Congo (DRC). The book attempts to determine the ancestry and reconstruct the history of this people using oral history and linguistic techniques.

The urge to want to know the past is not unique to the Bari. It has been an obsession of humankind since people began to live in settled groups. As Huntington (1997:21) puts it,

> "The most important distinctions among peoples are not ideological, political, or economic. They are cultural". Peoples and nations are attempting to answer the most basic question humans can face: Who are we? And they are answering that question in the traditional way human beings have answered it, by reference to the things that mean most for them. People define themselves in terms of ancestry, religion, language, history, values, customs and institutions. They identify with cultural groups: tribes, ethnic groups, religious communities, nations, and, at the broadest level, civilizations".

Basing his studies on recorded oral traditions as passed down from one generation to the next and with the help of historical comparative techniques, the author attempts to define who the Bari are, trace their ancestry and their migratory routes using oral tradition, language, religion, values, customs and institutions. As the author shows, Bari is a member of a larger language family known as Nilotic spoken in six African countries, namely: the Sudan, Ethiopia, Uganda, Kenya, Tanzania and the eastern part of the Democratic Republic of the Congo (DRC).

The Bari society is a preliterate community. Like the rest of the peoples of Africa, the history of the Bari lacks written historical tradition for all but the most recent centuries. All that exists is oral history and oral tradition. The author demonstrates that by employing linguistic and oral history methods, it is possible to write the history of a people without a written history. In that connection, in order to reconstruct the past history of the Bari, the author used comparative linguistic techniques to help corroborate the stories passed by word of mouth from generation to generation. The result has been impressive. Although a lot remains to be done, the author has helped the Bari to be aware of their history, with the help of this book.

Another merit of the study is that it is not only useful to the Bari but to the communities genetically related to the Bari as well. While talking about the Bari, the book has also shown that it is impossible to write a history of a people without having to refer to other neighbouring groups. For example, the last area the Bari left on their last push to the Nile Valley is a place called Lotuke, an area north east of lake Rudolf (present day Lake Turkana). Interestingly, the Toposa, Lango, Turkana, Lotuko and Maasai also claim this place to be their original homeland from where they dispersed to other areas.

The book also provides much needed explanation for what was a very confusing situation to me and I believe to others as well—the distinction between a Nilotic and a Nilo-Hamite. For a long time, I was made to understand that only the Dinka, Nuer, Shilluk, Dholuo, Acholi and the Anuak constituted the Nilotic language proper. Now the book shows that not only Bari but also even Lotuk and the Toposa are Nilotes! The question whether or not the so-called Nilo-Hamites were indeed also Nilotes or some other group was not clear. Indeed, are Nilotes also Hamites, or are Hamites Nilotes? The book tries to provide some answers to these difficult questions and much more. For example, the author points out that until recently, the Bari were thought to belong ethnically and culturally to a group of people known as Nilo-Hamites, a hybrid race made of half Nilotes and half Hamites. Oddly enough, the Nilotic group was itself regarded as a race of mixed affiliation. A mixture of what races was not clear, but probably a mixture of Semites, Hamites, Caucasians, Cushites, or Negroes.

What the author has done for Bari is commendable. One would wish that the same work were done on the other Nilotic languages in order to have a wider scope, and a comprehensive Nilotic history. It is only through doing in-depth study of the history of specific communities that one can hope to piece together what the history of these people was before dispersal. Such a study would provide the missing links in the whole jigsaw of unwritten past Nilotic history. However, until more research is conducted into the folktales, oral history, cultures and traditions of individuals to verify the veracity of these claims, they will remain just as myths.

An interesting claim made in the book is that the Bari, and by extension the other Nilotic peoples, migrated to their present site from a place further than the present day Khartoum in the Sudan; that the migration was largely from the North to the South. It is only by assuming a movement of the Nilotic peoples from the North to the South that can one account for the otherwise unexplainable linguistic, cultural and racial resemblances between these peoples. It would enable one to explain, for example, why Nubians in the far North, Bari in middle Sudan and the Maasai to the far south have remarkable racial, cultural and linguistic congruencies.

The ploy to dodge answering this question assumed two forms. One strategy was to claim that Nubian, Bari and Maasai (the so called Nilo-Hamites) borrowed heavily from a second language called 'Hemitic" which somehow then vanished without trace. The other position was to assume that these languages were, actually, originally Hamitic but then got so greatly influenced by Nilotics that they lost their unique Hamitic characteristics. Assuming any of these two positions does not require one to posit a theory of migration. To set the homeland of the Nilotic peoples further than the Bahr el Ghazal region and posit the possibility of movement of the Nilotic peoples, especially in North-South direction, is anathema to many Africanists.

The book is a huge contribution to the understanding of the history and culture of the Bari people. It shows that the Bari had a very rich past; that they also had a very tragic past. The larger portion of the nineteen-century was a period of monumental tragedy for the Bari people. There are very few communities that suffered more than the Bari in the process of colonization of the Sudan. Not only did the Bari lose most of its population and huge cattle wealth to the invaders, but also it was nearly wiped out.

I am sure both scholars and students of Bari culture and history will find the book extremely useful in their work. But for the first two technical chapters, the book makes very easy and interesting reading. The chaos that the Bari people went through during the one and half centuries of their history reminds one of the political and military corundum in the present day Western Upper Nile. I commend the book to you.

General Salva Kiir Mayar Dit
The President of the Government of Southern Sudan and
The First Vice President of the Republic of the Sudan

Khartoum, March 2007.

Acknowledgements

In a work of this kind, it is always impossible to acknowledge all but a few. Thus, though indebted to many people, I can directly thank only a few special people, foremost of whom are members of family; my wife Mary and children Rosalyn, Cathy and Vicky. I owe the children special thanks for being gracious enough and forgiving me for having taken time off from them in the most crucial period of their young lives to do many things unrelated to my parental duties. May the good Lord bless their kind souls.

My thanks also go to my colleagues and friends at the University of Nairobi, especially Godfrey Muriuki, Prof. Mohamed Abdulaziz and Kithaka Wa Mberia. Mberia for challenging me to write down something about the history of the Bari people rather than spend time doing esoteric syntax, which would not be accessible except to the most educated Bari; Godfrey Muriuki, who having read the first draft of the manuscript, literally ensured that I completed it. I thank him for the many tireless hours he took poring over the draft offering much valuable advice and making corrections. My gratitude also goes to the University of Nairobi Press for agreeing to be my publishers.

I also thank Anne Mumo of the School of Journalism. Anne did all the typesetting work and corrections. While in Khartoum, Anne was kind enough to keep me informed about the progress of the work. She coordinated between Prof. Muriuki, the publisher and I.

A work of this sort must always be triggered by a motivating force. This has been the curiosity of the enquiring minds of my little girls, Rosalyn, Cathy and Vicky, who having been born in exile, wanted to know who the Bari were. They would often ask their mother and I, "if the Bari were only found in the Sudan or whether there were other Bari people elsewhere". It is in an attempt to answer that question that I began to do some research on the question. The result is this book.

Introduction

What makes humans different from other species is their thirst to know their past. This past is important for their individual or collective self-esteem and is crucial in setting their present and future goals. The knowledge gained in the past by older generations is passed down to subsequent generations by word of mouth in preliterate societies or through the written form in literate communities.

This work is about an aspect of a people known as the Bari. The Bari society is a preliterate community. Like the rest of the peoples of Africa, the history of the Bari lacks written historical tradition for all but the most recent centuries. All that exists is oral history and oral tradition. With the rise of cultural and political chauvinism, there is a rising self-consciousness among people with unrecorded past to know what that past was. They are beginning to ask themselves soul-searching questions concerning their origins. For example, who are they? Who were their fore fathers? What were their achievements? Have they always lived in the places where they are now found, or have they come from elsewhere? If they moved to new places, what caused them to move? The Bari are also asking themselves similar questions.

Although it was a hotly contested issue until recently, it is now agreed by most scholars that the Bari belong ethnically and culturally to a people known as Nilotics. Much like the history of the rest of this people, their history is unwritten and, to all intents and purposes, buried deep in the sand dunes of history. For example, the Bari are not sure if the name Bari was the original name their ancestors used to call themselves by or not. Other than the general idea that they came to their present site from elsewhere, generally construed to be from the east, they did know where they came from.

Thus, part of this work is an attempt to suggest an answer to this difficult and daunting question. For the purposes of answering this question, and the further equally difficult issue regarding the racial and linguistic affiliation of the Bari people, the study examines linguistic theories and methodologies used in the past by scholars to analyse and classify languages, cultures, races, and origins of the peoples of Africa. Although these theories and methodologies were purported to be scientific, they were nothing more than mere stratagems for justifying making biased judgments and opinions about other peoples. Often, the conclusions arrived at using these techniques were *ad hoc* and inconsistent with the facts. What were presented as incontrovertible scientific facts were mere conjectures. For example, what are now called Nilotics were, until recently, taken to be a race of mixed affiliation. According to this school of thought, it was not clear whether or not the Nilotes were Semites,[1] Hamites, Caucasians, Cushites, Negroes or an admixture of all these races. However, the general informed opinion finally rested on the conclusion that this race may reasonably be divided into two large linguistic and racial groups namely: 'Nilotic' proper and the so-called, 'Nilo-Hamites'.

Language and race were taken to be conterminous. They were synonymous. The claim was that two communities that spoke two different languages belonged to two different races. Based on this classification, only the Nilotic proper would qualify to be of pure Negroid origin. The Nilo-Hamites would be classified as people of mixed race; half-Nilotic and half-Hamitic. Bari, Nubian and Maasai were alleged to be members of the later group.

We shall revisit the arguments that led to misclassification or cross-classification of what are obviously the same language and the same people into different races.[2] It should be pointed out, however, that the argument has already been made that the pure Nilotes and the Nilo-Hamites belong to one language family called Nilotic and one racial group-Negro. What has not, however, been established, and is still being contested, is their ancestral homeland. Where was the original home of the Nilotes? There are those who believe that the southern Sudan, especially around the Bahr el Ghazal Region, was the ancestral home of the Nilotes, at least the Luo of Kenya, (Ogot 1967).

We shall argue that this is only partly true. We shall claim that the Bahr el Ghazal region was not the epicenter of Nilotic migration. It was just another staging spot for further migration into the heart of the continent. We shall claim, contrary to established opinions, that the original home of the Nilotes, and by extension the Bari people, was further north, from the alleged Bahr el Ghazal area, but probably further north than the present northern Sudan. We shall argue that it was from this epicentre that the Nilotes swarmed out over time due to internecine wars and constant attacks by a relentless horde of marauding invaders from Asia and Europe and ecological change the drying up of the Sahara.

We shall claim further that the wide dispersal of the Nilotic peoples was due to migration; that the migration was largely from the north to the south.[3] It is only by assuming a movement of the Nilotic peoples from the north to south that can one account for the otherwise unexplainable linguistic, cultural and racial resemblances between these peoples. It would enable one to account, for example, why Nubians in the far north, Bari in middle Sudan and the Maasai to the far south of the African continent have remarkable racial, cultural and linguistic congruencies.

The ploy to dodge answering this question assumed two forms. One strategy was to claim that Nubians, Bari and Maasai (the so called Nilo-Hamites) borrowed heavily from a second language called 'Hemitic" which somehow then vanished without trace. The other position was to assume that these languages were, actually, originally Hamitic but then got so greatly influenced by Nilotic languages that they lost their unique Hamitic characteristics. Assuming any of these two positions does not require one to posit a theory of migration. To set the homeland of the Nilotic peoples further than the Bahr el Ghazal region and posit the possibility of movement of the Nilotic peoples, especially in north-south direction, is anathema to many Africanists.

There are those who religiously deny that the Nilotes have ever lived anywhere further than the bogs of southern Sudan. Nearly all scholars, and most of them western, would not hear of even a mere suggestion of a north-south migration of the Nilotes to their present homelands. If this thesis were to be admitted as a fact, what would prevent the further admission that, for example, the Luo, Dinka, Bari and the rest of their benighted lot came from, say Egypt? Now this is not such a good idea to western scholars. Egypt is the cradle of western civilization and it is unimaginable, if not outright impertinent, to suggest that such primitives as Bari or Maasai could have originated from there, let alone having participated in the development of that coveted civilization.

Although it will briefly touch on other areas of the Nilotics, the study will concentrate mainly on the Bari, especially what Spagnolo (1933) called 'proper Bari'. This is necessary because of matters of space and time. In any case, there are already important studies being done on the languages, cultures, and histories of individual Nilotic languages by scholars who belong to these languages, for example, Francis Deng on the Dinka and Bethwel Ogot on the Luo people. It is only by doing detailed work on individual Nilotic languages, histories and cultures that we shall be able to reconstruct the larger picture of Nilotics as a whole. The study of Bari is a contribution to that end.

Most of the information used in this study, particularly the part on the aspect of Bari history, come from oral and written sources. The written sources come from the early Europeans who came to Bariland in the early part of the 19th century and recorded, in writing, Bari oral history as they heard from the old speakers. These writings by explorers and missionaries, and later on the colonial administrators, have helped very greatly in the dating and the corroboration of the early history of the Bari people.

1

The Bari: Geographical Distribution

The Bari-speaking tribes are clustered together in the area south and southward of Mongolla, extending from latitude 6° 5´ down to latitude 3° 5´ on both sides of the Nile; all covering a length and breath of nearly 60 and 90 miles, respectively.

The Bari cluster of people are widely distributed in central Equatoria, otherwise known as Bahr el Gebel. The Bari proper live partly west and mostly east of the River Nile from between the Uma River in the south and Mongolla in the north. The *Fajulu* and the *Nyepo*[4] are found between Loka and Yei. The *Kuku* reside south of the Fajulu, towards the Uganda border. The Kakwa and the Ligi extend westwards from Yei into the Democratic Republic of the Congo (DRC) and into northern Uganda where there is a remnant of another Bari-speaking tribe, the *Kolubo*. The *Nyangwara* live north of the *Fajulu* and share borders with the *Mundari*, or the *Shir* as they are sometime known, and who are further north still and are spread to the east and the west of the Nile. To the north, these Bari-speaking tribes share the border with the Dinka Bor and the *Berri,* also known as *Peri*. To the east, they are surrounded by the Lulubö and the Sesere, two sub-tribes of the *Madi*; and further east still by the *Lokoya*; the *Lotuko* and the *Dongotono*, the languages of the two being closer to Bari. To the south-east are the *Acholi*. Westwards, the Bari are surrounded by almost a complete semi-circle of tribes speaking *Moru-Madi* dialects, such as *Avukaya, Logo, Kaliko, Lugbara* and *Madi*.

Socio-economic organization

In the past, the Bari were rigidly organized into a rigidly stratified community made up of freemen (*lui*), serfs (*tomonok*) and slaves (*'dupi*).[5] The Lui were the aristocratic upper class from amongst whom came the *Mor or rulers*, (*ko money kak*) or the chiefs of the land. The lui were further divided into those with rain (*kimaik ti pioŋ*) and those without rain (*bömön)* or rain chiefs.

Tomonok were of two types: *tomnok ti yukit* or artisans of the forge and *yari* or hunters. The *Yari* were further divided into two specialized groups, namely: the hunters of big game such as elephants, buffaloes, etc., known as the *Ligo* and *Tomonok ti kare* or river hunters. The *tomonok* constituted the middle tier of Bari social stratification. The first group among the *tomonok*, the *Yari*, hunted for the freemen. They lived apart from the Lui and away from the Nile in the open forest. They neither cultivated nor owned cattle. They lived on wild fruits, honey, termites (*koŋa*), *kite* or tamarind and mushrooms. They paid tribute of meat, honey, elephant tusks, and *kite lisi* (sweet tamarind) to their chief. When they wished to marry, they would come to their chief and beg him to assist them by giving the bull and the cow-calf *(tagwok)*, which was the customary bride-price of the servile classes. Like the *Yari*, *tomonok ti kare* also lived apart from the freemen, the *Lui*. They also lived apart form each other in separate villages according to their respective professions. Their huts were smaller than those of the freemen.

The job of the *tomonok ti yukit* (blacksmiths) was to make implements such as pottery, bowls, and arrows, hoes, spears, large hippopotamus harpoons *(koro)*, knives, trinkets and other tools required by the freemen. The second group are largely fishermen. They lived along the Nile and hunted for hippos, crocodiles, fish and other marine animals. Like the *Yari*, they paid tribute in the form of ten to fifteen hoes to the chief. Occasionally, they worked as domestic servants. They rarely intermarried with the freemen.

The lowest class in the Bari social order is the *'dupi* or *'dupi kaderak* (cooks). The *'dupi* are physically distinct from the Lui. They tended to be short, hairy, of reddish tinge and aged a lot faster than the average freemen according to Whitehead (1933:30). Their sole function was to cook for the freemen especially during social occasions. When a chief or wealthy noblemen died, he was often buried with his *'dupet*.

Against this background of specialized occupational classes stood the *Lui* or the freemen, representing the superior cattle-owning element of Bari society. The ownership of cattle, the 'possession of the principal posts of the state and general sense of superiority, marked them off from the servile classes' (Whitehead 1933). Not all freemen had cattle but even poor freemen did not run the risk of becoming serfs. It should be pointed out, however, that as in much of African history, the division of society into slave, free and immigrant conquerors and the conquered autochthonous is common practice.

Pastoral life

Cattle were central to the social and economic life of the Bari people. Life without cattle was unthinkable. A man judged to be rich or poor depending on whether he possessed cattle or not. The possession of cattle conferred great social prestige. It was only through the payment of sufficient cattle that a creditable marriage could be achieved. The poor suitor laid himself open to all sorts of taunts and insults (Whitehead 1962:131). The organization and the working life of the community from dawn to dusk revolve around the cow as White head reports:

> "In the morning the cows are driven out to the pasturage near the village (*ratet na toro'bo*); at midday they are driven back to the village, and rest during the heat of the day under the village tree; it is during this time that they are milked. Cows, however, which have just calved, are not milked for about a month; then as the calves grow bigger, they are deprived of some of the milk and the cows are milked at bout 5 a.m. When the calves no longer need milk, the cows return to the usual routine of midday milking. After a midday rest, they are driven out once more to the pasturage. Men of all ages milk; old men, young men and boys. If there is a domestic serf in the household, it falls on him to milk the cows" (Whitehead 1962:139).

Kurumi (cattle camp) was the centre of activity for that is where the bulk of the young men are occupied. Until the Bari lost their cattle and nearly all of its population to a horde of rapacious invaders who ravaged their country for the greater part of the 19th and early parts of the 20th centuries, they did little cultivation. After the harvest had been gathered, and as the dry season approached, the young and the active men of the village drove off the cattle to some place where more ample supplies of water and still unburned grass were to be found. The cattle and their herds would remain in this dry season kraal for about four months, December or January to March or April. There, a *kurumi* or large cattle enclosure was built of posts of ebony wood and thorns. The *teton* or young men of between eighteen and thirty five years of age, remained in the cattle camp, while the married men, women and children stayed at home, and the young girls journeyed backwards and forwards carrying milk.[6]

The warriors herded the cattle by day and danced and sang by night. Their food for the most part consisted of blood drawn from the necks of bulls and mixed with milk and a little flour. At the end of the dry season and the beginning of the rainy season, the cattle were returned home. Their return to the permanent village was a big occasion celebrated by a big dance.

During their stay at the *kurumi*, the young men kept themselves fully occupied. When they were not herding, milking, dancing and singing or fighting off wild animals from attacking their cattle, they were hunting for reed rats or raiding for cattle from their neighbours. The young men and young women were organized into age sets known as *ber* – similar to the Maasai *moran*. They went through the initiation rite of passage when they became of age. The women wore animal skins and they anointed themselves with red iron powder called *meje*, or ochre.

Cattle wealth was equitably distributed between members of the family and or clan. The cattle were divided into (a) *kɩsuk lomoriot* (cattle that are exclusively owned by the head of the household), (b) *kɩsuk matiat* (cattle that will provide milk), (c) *kɩsuk yɛmɛsi* (cattle for marriage).

The cattle that a man had acquired in exchange for *dura,* or money, were not shared by the family or clan. They were exclusively his and were thus called *kɩsuk matiat*, from the word *lomore,* meaning private. However, a man may have the right of use without the enjoyment of complete control. The cows are just for the purpose of providing him with milk. These are *kısuk lomoriot*. As Whitehead (1962) noted, if a man helped another to build a kraal or to herd his cattle, he had a cow assigned to him whose milk he could use, and at its death he could perhaps get its horns and hide as well. But the beneficiary was responsible for the animal; if it was killed, he had to satisfy its owner as to what become of it by bringing him its hide with the cattle marks upon its ears. A rich or influential man could build up a circle of hangers-on (known as *kalipönök*) from such recipients of his patronage (Whitehead 1962:140).[7]

Nearly all cows are *kısuk yemesi* or *nyeresi*—cattle for bride wealth. Most of the cattle in this category are cows from the marriage of daughters. The father of the family generally administers such cows. Out of this common wealth, some claims are paid outright. The father of the family remains in nominal control. Cattle from bride wealth are distributed among the family as follows:[8]

- Cow and cow-calf to the bride's mother.
- Cow and a bull-calf to bride's father.
- Bull for breeding.
- Favourite ox (dwöt sönö).
- Cattle of the herd (kısuk ti teŋ).
- Calf (tagwok na mananye) mother's brother.
- Cows (kısuk kölöt) father's brothers.

The father of the bride has the bulk of the bride-price cattle. The *kısuk ti teŋ* are not in some sense his own property to do what he likes with. He holds the cows as a trust which he administers for the benefit of the other members of the family. For instance, he assigns some of the cows to other wives to provide milk for them and their children; when his daughter for whom he received these cattle bears a child, he will hand over some of the wealth to her. His sons will also be entitled to some of it, either to provide them with milk, or to furnish them with the bride-wealth which they must hand over when they come to marry. A young man wishing to marry may do so because he does not need to have personal wealth. Marriage is a collective family responsibility.[9] It is the father and the father's brother, or clan members (*lokikolan*), who carry out the whole marriage negotiations. The marriage negotiation, known as '*putet*', determines the obligations and liabilities of the bridegroom's relatives and the claims and rights of the bride's relatives. Special 'bond' cows are paid to the mother of the bride, and uterine brother known as *kiteŋ moken ko tagwok* (a cow and a heifer) and *kiteŋ mananyɛ ko tore a dwöt (*a cow and male calf).[10]

A chief or a rich man may pay as many as 500 head of cattle or more. At the end of the century, 10 to 15 cows would be all that a rich man would expect to pay, and very often less.

Cattle ownership amongst the Bari people is not, in the words of Whitehead (1962:142), an 'unfettered private ownership'. Rather, it is a trust. Consequently, inheritance is nothing more than the passing of this trust to the next head of the family. It may be the man's eldest son, or in the case where the family is still young, his brother.

In common with other Nilotic tribes, the Bari think very highly of their herd of cattle. A man must have a special favorite bull known as the *dwöt sönök* to represent his individuality. The *sönö* is chosen for its colouring and its horns are trained to grow in a particular fashion, much like what the Dinka do today. This was called '*dulö na ongwara*', or twisting of the horns.[11] Such a bull was well fed and groomed and was the source of pride for the owner and the whole family. The horns were softened by applying the fruit of heated *uŋuguli*—sausage-fruit (Kigelia) on it. It was then twisted into the desired shape. Often, it was sharpened to enable the bull to defend itself and the herd against predators. When at the *kurumi* and nothing much was going on, sometimes these favourite oxen were incited to fight each other by their respective owners.

A man chooses his *sönö* when he reaches the ages of between 27 and 30 and when he has enough cattle. When he has selected his favourite bull, he composes a song, or more often, he takes a goat as a gift to a renown poet who would then compose a personal song for him, known as *köli gotet.* That done, he prepares a feast of beer and invites his *bɛr* (age mates), and together he takes them through the phases of reciting his song. When he is satisfied that his age-mates have mastered the song thoroughly, it is then sung in a public dance.

The *sönö* is never killed for frivolous reasons. Often, it is allowed to outlive the owner and remains as a memorial of him to their families. In the event that a man wants to replace his old *sonö* with a young one, he gives instructions to slay the old one but then he must show great sorrow. He must go into mourning, refrain from eating any of the meat of the bull, and remain in seclusion in his house for sometime. It is almost as if one of his sons had died.

Oft-times, as the men tend their cattle at mid-day under a large tree (*toket*) in the village, the proud owner of an ox would sprinkle white sand upon its back, give it milk to drink and boast of its merits—*wursuk* (a sneeze). The owner would say; "The horns of my father are dappled, red, black and so on or the horns of father's bull are twisted" (Whitehead 1962:142). These are called *polesi*.[12]

This kind of treatment forges a very close bond between the animal and its owner. 'If misfortune befalls the ox, and it is captured by cattle raiders, its owner will go to great lengths to recover it, while the animal will leap a kraal hedge in answer to its master's call as Baker and his forty thieves found out on their seize and *ghazwe* they carried out in Bilinyang (Baker 1871:163–164).[13]

Agriculture

As we have seen above, much of the life of the Bari revolved around cattle. There was very little cultivation done and mostly it involved old people around the hut. Generally, the food crops shown in Table 1 were grown.[14]

Sörömöndi (groundnuts) and *Bömuk* (maize) are probably later additions to the Bari diet.[15]

The main crop of the whole area was the dura. There are three types of dura; (a) the *kigo* or the red dura. It has a hard seed, which is resistant to attack of the dura birds; (b) the *Kigo*, which is sown with *leyot* between June and September. The crops were not sown in any order but maize is always grown early. It was possible to get two crops with the exception of the white *dura* which takes up to nine months to yield harvest. After the first six months or six weeks after the onset of the rainy season, the two activities of sowing and harvesting go on hand in hand until the end of the wet period.

Table 1: *Food crops grown in Bari*

Native Name	English Name	Scientific Name
Könyuŋ	Simsim	Sesamum indicum Linn
Kinu	Hyptis spicigera	
Loputu	Beans	Vigna nolotica
Logwu'dik	Beans	Longocarpus laxiflorus
Leyot	Eleusine	Eleusine Coracana
Kigo	Dura	
Kalu	Yam	Helmia bulbifera
Bekaya	Yam	Dioscorea sativa Linn.
Monduru	A kind of simsim	Sesamum indicum
Kuluji	Marrow	Cucumis tinneana

Men dig and sow while women do the weeding and harvesting. Often, the cultivation was done in a '*mole*' (group cultivation). The man, whose garden is being prepared, brews beer and cooks food. He then invites the men to help him in the cultivation of his garden.

Ownership of gardens and allocation of produce

The wife and her offspring own the produce of the garden. Each garden that a man cultivates is allocated to a particular wife, if the man has more than one wife, which is more often the case. On the death of the husband, the man who inherits her also takes charge of the gardens and the raising of food supply for the family of the deceased.

The man always cultivates one especial garden for his private use only, known as '*melesen lomore.*' Even as a young unmarried man, a Bari man begins to cultivate his *melesen lomore* and uses the produce to exchange for goats or sheep. When he is married, Whitehead reports that a Bari still keeps his private garden and its produce is now used for feeding strangers *'kömu'*, for use during famine, and for providing grain for use in ritual purposes. This garden is known variously as *melesen na ngun,* (garden of God), *melesen na mulö* or *melesen na miyan* (the garden of spirits).

Harvesting was a time of plenty and joy for the whole village. It is the time for showing gratitude and offering sacrifices to the gods and the spirits of the dead, much in the spirit of the ancient Greeks and Romans. Ceremonies that relate to the produce of the field are the duty of women and are known as *'waju'*. Those that include the offering of meat are called *'rubaŋgajin'* and are conducted by men. The offerings are made three times in the year, from *'bolot'*, (duara), *'leyot'* (elsine) and *'loputu'* (beans).

There are two seasons that determine the Bari rhythm of life: the wet and the rainy seasons. The rainy months of the year are from April to October. Rainfall increases steadily until it reaches its peak in between July and August and begins to decline around October. The Bari encodes these fluctuations in rain distribution in names. These are:[16]

- *Meliŋ*: the dry season lasting from October to March.
- *Kiser*: 'the beginning of the rainy season, from March to April.
- *Ja'be*: the early part of the rainy season from may to June.
- *'Butun*: the harvest season from June or July to September or October.

As for months, the Bari apply the same naming system they use for naming their children to months, at least the first four months of the year. The other months are merely given descriptive labels as shown in Table 2.

Table 2: *System of naming calendar months in Bari*

1.	*Yugusuk*	First born	January
2.	*Laduya*	Second birth	February
3.	*Wani Mamaya*	Third born (roasted)	March
4.	*Pitya*	Fourth born	April
5.	*Mariŋ*	Fifth born	May
6.	*'Baka*	First cultivation ended	June
7.	*'Dogale Rube*		July
8.	*Nylekundya*		August
9.	*Bojo*		September (plenty of food)
10.	*Daŋpiru*		October
11.	*Atupa*		November (divided into two)
12.	*Mökik*		December

2

Language Family

For quite sometime, there has been a major confusion and uncertainty about the linguistic and racial affiliation of the Bari people. That is true of other peoples of Africa. Often, and depending on the methodology employed, one gets the strange spectacle of one group of people being crossed-classified into one or more ethnic or racial types.

At one time, the Bari people were believed to belong to a mixed race of people made up of Nilotes and Hamites, the so-called Nilo-Hamites. However, there were those who thought the Bari were nothing, but a Negroid-Nilotic people. Yet others were of the opinion that the Bari were a lost race of Hamites or Caucasians in the heart of Africa.

For a very long time, the study of Africa, the ethnic and linguistic classification of its peoples, cultures and histories have been the preserve of Africanist scholars. Nearly all of these scholars were none Africans and were largely anthropologists, anthropological historians and historical linguists. Much 28307 of the work has been written within the theoretical framework of their own ethnology; and historians and others have relied almost entirely on the classification of peoples by anthropologists (Williams 1976: 190).

In this chapter, we examine the theoretical and methodological under-pinnings that were used in the classification of African languages and the controversies arising therein, with a view to understanding and assessing the credibility of the claims made about racial or linguistic affiliations of peoples using these theories and methodologies. It is important to revisit the theories and methodologies because it will help us in understanding the refutations and claims that will be made about the origin, linguistic and racial affiliations of the Nilotic peoples, including the Bari people. It will be seen, for example, that at one time or another, the Bari and the Maasai have been cross-classified as belonging to all sorts of races or language groups: Hamitic, a hybrid race (Nilo-Hamitic) or Negroid-Nilotic. Although this classification has been revised, this information is still not current. It is, therefore, important that people are made aware of this fact.

This classification came at a time when science, especially in the natural sciences and biology, was making rapid advances. Not to be left behind, social scientists followed suit. Linguists were among the first to apply scientific theories in their study of human languages. Borrowing from 19th century biologists, most especially from Darwin's theory of evolution, linguists believed that differences and resemblances between human languages or groups of languages might be accounted for by using the same theory. Darwin's theory of evolution holds that all biological organisms must either adapt or perish for survival. Linguists assumed this to be true of human languages as well. Like any biological organism, language too must adapt and change overtime.

But for a few variations, there are two broad versions of evolutionary theories: creationism and transformationism. Creationism holds that all things are unchangeable and that but for a few haphazard modifications, things have remained unaltered since they came to be through a single act of creation. In its extreme form, this view holds that all forms are related by common origin. The idea is that there was a single primeval form from which all others developed. This was also known as monogenesis theory. Thus, it is enough to assume that the result of variation or common resemblances of certain languages to one another is nothing else but a result of evolutionary change of one common ancestral language mutating into other related languages. In its simplest form, the theory of evolution presupposes a common descent. In addition, this is the fundamental hypothesis underlying the concept of genetic relationships among languages.

The theory of genetic evolution of human languages gained empirical support when it yielded spectacular results in the study of Indo-European and Semitic languages in the early part of the nineteenth century. Evidence at the time led and still leads to the polygenetic theory of evolution since not all languages can be demonstrated to have a common origin, unless one believed in the 'Tower of Babel's' story in the Bible. However, the assumptions of a similar process of differentiation for an earlier period and the absence of any proof of spontaneous generation in historic times lend plausibility to the speculation of monogenesis.

A less extreme version of the monogenetic theory is termed transformationism. The transformationists assume that each existing form is connected with at least some forms but not with all forms as a result of distinct creations. Connecting forms among some phyla, for which plausible common ancestry cannot at present be found, are claimed to be accounted for by this monogenetic version of trans-formationism. This position is, however, refuted by those who subscribe to polygenetic version of creationism by pointing out that one can assume the existence of several creations where links cannot be established without denying that the species are fixed types.

A more extreme form of the transformationist theory postulates that all existing forms are historically connected by a dynamic process of growth: the greater the similarity among existing forms, the more recent the common ancestry. It further assumes that all forms were connected by descent and that common ancestors are forms different from any existing forms today and gave rise to present forms through a process of differential and independent development. Because change is gradual and coherent, it allowed for minor leaps as, for example, those induced by the process of mutation in cell biology.

A third theory known as catastrophism, popular with 19th century geologists, holds that from time to time, all species are destroyed and new ones are created without affiliation by descent from forms of the previous area. This theory denies that relation exists between dead species and new forms. The same is true of human languages. When a language dies, a new one is born in its place and the dead language and the new one do not have to be related at all.

In summary, change and, therefore, diversity can come about in any of the four ways, through: (a) evolutionary monogenesis (b) evolutionary polygenetic (c) creation and (d) evolutionary catastrophic change.

The three theories were the main frameworks used by anthropologists and linguists in their study and classification of languages, including African languages. These theories gave rise to different methodologies. As will become clear, the use of these theories and attendant methodologies led to all sorts of often conflicting conclusions. In addition to the assumption about the origin of language, linguists also use the following three methods to categorize and classify languages. Languages are related either genetically, by areal or typological features. The accuracy and validity of a classification depended on the method or combination of methods employed.

The first to apply evolutionary theory to the study of languages was August Schleicher (1863).[17] August Schleicher was a leading linguist of the nineteenth century who recognized the likeness between genetic relationship and the evolutionary process in biology. He posited three stages in language evolution: (a) the isolating stage where each word is just a single morpheme, (b) the agglutinating or a multi-morphemic stage and (c) the inflectional stage, where irregular and complex forms appear in the language. It was assumed that the simpler the morphology of the language, the more primitive the language is.

Language development is assumed to evolve from the isolating, which is the most primitive, to agglutinating, considered to be a little more developed than the inflectional type, which is held to be the most developed. The development of the language was held also to reflect the stage of development of the speakers of the language. Case and gender marking, too, were alleged to be additional indicators of developed languages. It was held that a people who spoke isolation languages were a little more primitive than a people who spoke the other types of languages. Therefore, less primitive peoples spoke agglutinating languages and the most advanced races, mostly western peoples, spoke inflectional languages, marked off by an additional use of gender and case. It was alleged that these facts were clearly shown in such advanced human languages as Sanskrit, Latin, German and old English.

Genetic classification

Genetically related languages are languages that are assumed to have originated from a common ancestor. Genetic classification therefore is taken to reflect historical events that must have occurred. Such classification is based on sound-meaning resemblances of linguistic forms. The languages under consideration do not necessarily have to be in one geographical area, although in general, related languages tend to be found within one general location, though not necessarily in continuous distribution. English is a good illustration. English has spread and is currently being spoken across four continents. Were people to be discovered on some planet speaking a language with the vocabulary and grammar of English, a common genetic relationship would have to be assumed, regardless of geographical circumstances.

Typological classification

Typological analysis compares sound without meaning, meaning without sound or both. Using the sound or phonetic criterion only, for example, the languages of the world may be divided into two broad groups: (a) those with tonal systems and (b) those without tonal systems. One may also use a semantic feature. Using a semantic feature only, one might divide the languages of the world into those that have morphemes indicating sex and gender and those which do not. We could then, for example, combine the two criteria above, tone and gender, to produce four classes of languages: (a) tonal-gender, (b) non-tonal-gender, (c) non-tonal-non-gender and (d) gender-non-gender.

Word order is also another typological feature. Languages may be either subject and object (so called verb initial language) verb (SVO) and verb, subject and object, (the so called verb-final tags) (VSO) or any other combination (Nyombe 1996; Greenberg 1963). As Greenberg (1957:67) points out, 'typological classifications are arbitrary because any criterion or combination of criterion may be used with consistent results, provided that only they have clear meaning when applied to diverse languages.'

Areal classification

Areal classification considers effects of one language or languages upon one another, whether or not they are related. Among the relevant data to be considered in such classification are borrowing, involving both sound and meaning and influences in sound only or in meaning only which are a result of historical contact. A number of languages found to share the same features may be termed 'areal group' languages. Furthermore, areal classification rely more on judgments as to whether or not one language is influenced by another and to what extent. Generally speaking, group languages are geographically continuous. Due to their contiguity, areal languages always influence each other through lexical borrowing. Although accident cannot be ruled out, this phenomenon largely points to the fact that borrowing between the same languages within the same semantic range, geographical proximity and the existence of other non-linguistic evidence of cultural contact is not accidental.

Diffusion and migration

Another theory that is held to explain cultural relation or resemblances between groups of languages is diffusion. Diffusion theory assumes that cultural resemblances between cultural areas exist due to historical connection originating in the movement of cultural features. In that regard, it is akin to theories of migration that sought to explicate cultural and linguistic resemblances in terms of movement of peoples. As a matter of fact, diffusionist concepts are often treated as equivalent to migration theories.

A diffusionist school known as the Kulturkresis or the 'cultural circle' (Graebner 1911 and Schmidt 1939 among others) was the foremost proponents of this concept. The leaders of this school were; Akermann, Foy, Schmidt and Koppers. This school held that kulturkresis may be accounted for on the basis of cultural features such as Quality and Quantity. Quality compares two or more individual traits that represent the same trait. For each individual trait such as say, a house type, a qualitative comparison will distinguish features that are independent of one another and not determined by the function of the material trait or institution. For example, a house type can be compared on the basis of say: the ground plan, material used for constructing it, the form of the roof, types of decorations, the number and kinds of entrances to it, and so on. Now, if a number of such qualitative similarities are found, a common historical connection can be established.

Quantitative concept refers to the presence of convincing qualitative resemblances in a number of different traits of a culture. The purpose of the quantitative criterion is to reinforce the resemblances established by the qualitative method. The application of the qualitative criterion strengthens the case of each of the qualitative resemblances- a sort of hindsight, fail-safe mechanism.

The problem with this methodology is that it is perfectly possible that two independent peoples might arrive at exactly similar, for example, house types, which share the same number of qualitative similarities. The proponents of the theory counter that chance can be eliminated by positing a series of different traits of say, for example, house types, weapons, musical instruments, social organizations, religions and so on. Even so, this view still suffers from the weakness that it is too broad. Based on these concepts, it is possible to establish cultural relation across various disparate parts of the world for example Asia, Oceania, Africa and South America. How would the proponents of this theory account for this? Their only recourse would be to posit an implausible series of migrations. However, used in conjunction with other theories such as the evolutionary theory, it can yield some surprising result.

Having examined the assumptions, theories and methodologies used in the study of languages, let us now look closely at how Africanist researchers have used these tools to categorize African peoples and languages and their cultures, paying particular attention to Nilotic languages, especially how the Bari have been classified.

From the literature, African languages have largely been grouped into two broad language families and an admixture of races namely: (1) Afro-Asiatic and (2) Nilo-Saharan. The Nilo-Saharan family has other sub-families among which are the so called Nilotic group of languages. African languages have been willy-nilly classified as belonging to one or other of these groups. Often, linguists are not even agreed on each other's classification. What is called Nilotic is considered to be a member of the Eastern-Sudanic axis of the larger Nilo-Saharan family. Until recently, for example, linguists, anthropologists and historians were not agreed on whether or not what are termed Nilotes are, in fact, "Nilotes", Hamites, Cushites, Negroes, Semites, Caucasian or an admixture of these races. As the researchers were uncertain about the ethnicity of these peoples, so were they equally unable to determine the original ancestral homeland of the Nilotes. In fact, even today, historians are still undecided whether or not indeed the Nilotes are of one race or a mixture of races.

Although the Nilotes are found over a wide geographical spread, some of these scholars argue that this does necessarily mean that these people belong to the same racial group. Rather, the regular linguistic and cultural correspondences evident in this group of languages are due to diffusion and borrowing of linguistic forms and cultural features from other contiguous groups.

3
Language and Race

Among the first to study and attempt to classify Nilotic languages and the race of people who speak them was L. Reinisch (1879). In his "Die sprachliche stellung des Nuba", Reinsch postulated that the languages spoken around the Lake Tana area in Ethiopia languages - such as Dembea, Quara, Agaumeder and others—constituted the closest links to Nubian and that these languages were essentially Hamitic. That being the case, he concluded that the speakers of these languages are Hamites. Reinisch argued that since Nubian also constitutes a link between the Hamitic languages which includes such Nilotic languages as Dinka, Nuer and Shilluk he deduced that the owners of these languages were also Hamites. Thus, Reinisch attributed a Hamitic origin to these people of the Nile Valley. Reinsch here adopted an evolutionary framework and assumed that Nilotes were, in fact, descendants of Hamites.

Another attempt comes from Meinhof (1912) who partially agrees with Reinsch thesis that Nilo-Hamitic languages were essentially Hamitic, but singles out Bari and Maasai as being the only ones of the group who are really originally Hamitic; and that these languages got eventually heavily influenced by Nilotic languages. While appearing to agree with Reinsch, Meinhof is, in fact, making a much more serious allegation; that Hamitic and the Hamites belong to different language group and are members of a different race from the Nilotes. There are thus two races, Nilotes and Hamites. This raises a problem and a riddle. If the Nilotes are Negroes by assumption, what is and what was the race of the Hamites? Where did they live? We will attempt to answer these questions below.

Oblivious to this glaring contradiction, Westermann (1912) sided with Reinsch but renamed Reinsch Nilotic as Niloto-Sudanic. Dinka, Nuer, Shilluk, Acholi, Luo together with an assortment of other West African languages belonged to this group. Bari, Maasai and Nubian constituted his second category—the Niloto-Hamitic language family or ethnic group. It is important to bear in mind that language and race were construed to be synonymous. These terms were quite often used in free variation, language for race and race for language. Westermann argues that the Niloto-Hamitic languages, most especially Bari and Maasai—together with such related languages as, Suk, Nandi, Turkana, Lotuho to mention but a few—exhibited heavy foreign influences, largely Hamitic to which they had been exposed. Thus Westermann does not accept a common Hamitic origin of the Nilotic. He even does not accept the classification of Nubian as Hamitic. According to him, the Hamitic influences found in Nubian, Bari and Maasai are a result of massive borrowing from Hamitic. So the line between Niloto-Sudanic and Niloto-Hamitic is not easy to define; they all have components of Sudanic and Hamitic origin, only that in some cases the first is prevalent, in others, the latter. Again, here, what is assumed but not explained is the term Hamitic. Is it a linguistic or racial designation? If it is a racial epithet, what race does it designate, Negro, Semitic or Caucasian? The same lack of clarity arises with the word Sudanic.

Unlike, Westermann, Murray and Roy (1920) postulated that the Niloto-Sudanic and Niloto-Hamitic languages of Westermann, including Nubian, belonged to the same language family in the remote past but that these were later permeated with Hamitic influences. They postulated that this language family was essentially Nilotic, not Hamitic. Thus there are largely two groups—Nilotic and Hamitic. All the Niloto-Sudanic and Nilo-Hamitic groups of Reinch, Westermann and Meinhof are collapsed into one group—Nilotic. This group includes, Nubian, Bari, Maasai, Dinka, Nuer, Shilluk, Lotuho, Teso and so on.

However, in spite of the simplification in the classification, Murray and Roy still found the classification of Bari, Nubian and Maasai troublesome. For some reason, Bari, Nubian and Maasai resembled Hamitic more rather than Nilotic. Why was this the case? The reason they gave for this was that, although these languages were originally Nilotic, they became so heavily permeated with Hamitic influences that their Nilotic origins have, to a large extent been lost. They hypothesized that the Nilotic language family belonged to what he termed 'the Southern Branch' of the larger branch of his 'Eastern Sudanic' branch of Nilo-Saharan. The Eastern Sudanic branch of Nilo-Saharan is made of Nubian, Beir-Didinga, Barea, Tabi, Merarit, Dagu and the Southern Nilotic branch to which Nilotic belongs. He divided Southern Nilotic into, (a) Nilotic and (b) Great Lakes languages-Westermann's Nilito-Hamito group.

He classified Nilotic into three subfamilies, namely: (a) Burun (b) the Luo group (Shilluk, Anuak, Acholi, Alur, Chopi, Lango, Jaluo and Luo) (c) Dinka and Nuer. The Great Lakes languages consists of two branches: (a) the Bari group, (Bari, Mundari, Pajulu, Kakwa, Nyangwara, Kuku) Maasai, Teso, Lotuho, Turkana, Toposa, and Karimojong, (b) Nandi-Suk. Greenberg replaced the Niloto-Hamitic term 'the Great Lakes" languages. He noted that lexical comparison of the Great Lakes and the Nilotic languages 'reveal vocabulary resemblances in fundamental noun, adjective, and verb stems that are so obvious and extensive in number that it would be pointless to enumerate them' (Greenberg 1950:143). Many authors have simply discounted these resemblances in favor of supposed Hamitic features in morphology. In Greenberg's view, the large number of vocabulary items common to the Nilotic and the Great Lakes languages seem sufficient to prove genetic relationship of the two groups beyond any reasonable doubt. This being the case, he wonders why what he called the Great Lakes languages were called Nilo-Hamitic by many authors. He dismissed the so called Nilo-Hamitic theory.[18]

Proponents of the Hamitic theory have used the term Nilo-Hamitic with such widely varying meanings that the term has almost become meaningless. According to Greenberg, 'it seems to have all things to all men'. Bernhard Struck (1911), for example, accepted Meinhof's thesis that these languages were Hamitic pure and simple. They were Hamitic languages in Nilotic area. "...the term Nilo-Hamitic indicates in a very appropriate manner the Hamites inhabiting the Nile valley in a north-south direction". Similarly the anthropologist C.G. Seligman (1934) thought the so-called Nilo-Hamites were, in fact, Half-Hamites—a Negro admixture. A.N. Tucker (1963) thought that the Nilo-Hamitic languages were a hybrid group of languages made up of three defined characteristics: (a) a large common vocabulary of noun stems; (b) a large common vocabulary of non-Nilotic stems and (c) a large common vocabulary of Hamitic-like prefixes and suffixes.

Broadly speaking, opinions regarding the classification of Nilotic languages may be divided into two broad groups: those who believed that the Nilo-Hamitic, or Great Lakes languages were Hamitic and those who thought that the Nilo-Hamitic languages were Nilotic but had undergone Hamitic structural change to the point where they must be considered a kind of linguistic hybrid.

Murray and Leroy (1920), were among a few who gave empirical data in support of their contention that Bari and Nubian were either Hamitic or were heavily influenced by Hamitic. They gave some substantive and structural resemblances in Bari and Nubian, which they believed to have been borrowed from Hamitic. In their study of verb forms, they observed that:

> "At first sight, the Nubian verb, which has personal endings, differs remarkably from the Bari verb, which is not, and the methods of tense formation also differ—Nubian suffixes, Bari reduplicates. But both verbs possess in common a remarkable system of extending the meaning of the verbal root by means of suffixes,"[19] The paradigms in Table 3 below show Bari and Nubian resemblance.

Table 3: *Bari and Nubian verbal roots*

English	Nubian	(Kenus, Dogola dialects)	Bari Meaning
Root	Bog	'buk	Pour
Imperative	Bog-u	'buk-é	Pour
Inchoative	Bog-an	'buk-ö(n)	To become poured
Reflexive	Bog-ji	'bukö-ji	Pour for oneself
Intensive	Bog-ir	'buk-örö	Pour away
Causative	Bog-kid	'bukö-kin	Pour for some one
Instrument	Bog-ad	'buk-et	Something for pouring
Agent	a-bog-il	Ka-'bukö-nit	One who pours
Infinitive used as a substantive	Bog-an	'buk-ö	To pour

One thing one immediately notices between the Nubian and the Bari forms is their semantic congruence. Observe that the forms have exactly the same meaning in the two languages. There are phonetic differences between the forms, however. While the final root consonants in the Nubian forms are voiced, the Bari forms are voiceless. This could be attributed to an intervocalic voicing rule in Nubian, where a voiceless velar stop becomes voiced when it occurs between vowels. Final stops voicelessness in Bari is due to an opposite general phonological rule that devoices final voiced bilabial plosives.

Like Mitterrutzner (1919), they considered the suffixes (-in, -bu, -du) in the Bari forms below as aspects of assimilation, captured by a simple formal phonological rule:

[r]————>[d] /n————#

The rule merely states that the consonant /r/ becomes /d/ when it is preceded by the nasal consonant /n/.

- rem-bu 'to slay'
- göm-bu 'to surround'
- rem-ru 'to throw away from the speaker'
- göm-ru 'to surround away from the speaker'
- gwad-du 'to sprinkle with water'
- baran-du 'to overflow'

Thus, *ai gen-ri* is realized as *ai gen-di* and occasionally after /r/ as *ted-de* for *ter-re* in Dogolawi. According to them, this was ample proof that the same assimilations also occurred in Nubian as attested by the following forms:

- tomb 'to break to pieces'
- gend 'reconcile'

The underlying forms of these roots are [tom], and [gen]. When the suffix /–r/ is added to these forms, gen-ri, and tom-r, they are realized as/gend/ and /tom-b/

In the area of substantives, Murray and Roy alleged that Nubian substantive possessed case-endings derived from Hamitic languages which Bari substantive somehow lost or never possessed. What was considered important here was their resemblance in the method of plural formation.

Formation of the plural from the singular

Bari like Maasai, has a multiplicity of plural suffixes which are grouped into three:

(a) –k: ku–

In 'nomina agentis', the singular of which is /–nit/, /–nit/ is dropped in the plural and replaced by /–k/:

Ka-remo-nit 'murderer'	ka-remo-k' murderers';
Ka-todinö-nit' teacher'	ka-todinö-k' teachers';

Certain nouns and pronouns of relationship prefix /ko–/ and '/ku–/:

baba' father'	ko-baba 'fathers'
yango 'mother'	ko-yango 'mothers'
'lu' 'that' (masc)	ku-lu 'those' (masc)

(b) –t, –at, –et, –ot, –at, etc

The vowel height in (b) is determined by the root of the form to which it is prefixed by a phonological process known as vowel harmony. Examples are:

Kuŋu 'knee'	kungu-at 'knees'
aburi 'gazelle'	aburi-et 'gazelles'
yöbu 'forest	yöbu-öt 'forests'

(c) –a(n), –e(n), –o(n), –ö(n)

The parenthesis indicates that the final nasal consonant is sometimes elided:

bar 'flood'	bar-a(n) 'floods'
keŋe 'dwarf'	keŋe-lon 'dwarfs'
jur 'land'	jur-ön 'lands

(d) –ji, –jin, –ji, –ki, –kin, –la, –lan, etc.

These too and many others, probably compounds of the above, are employed in plural formation.

The suffixes –k, –t and –n appear also in Maasai and Shilluk. According to these writers (Murray and Roy 1920:261–270), they probably originally 'represented classes such as perhaps, men, beasts, things and that in spreading from one language to another their original significance have been lost sight of'. Meinhof claimed to have the same forms in Nama where they represent masculine, feminine and common grammatical genders. Murray and Roy claim that the suffixes described above can be or are also found in Hamitic languages.

Formation of the singular from the plural

The method of forming the singular from the plural in Bari is different from Hamitic, and appears to be' peculiarly Nilotic. The plural suffix /-k/ may be regarded as having a singular suffix /–nit/ since the later does not appear in the plural. The other singularitivizer suffixes: –tat, –tot, –töt, –tet; –ti and many others, (cf. Spangolo 1933) were, in fact, originally diminutives.

Pioŋ 'water'	pioŋ-tot'	a drop of water'
Jogi 'beeds'	jogi-tat'	'a beed'
Löɲi, 'berries'	löɲi-töt'	a berry'
Kalogo 'weaver birds'	kalugu-ti	'an weaver bird'

The article

Murray and Roy points out that traces of the Maasai article appear clearly in Bari and less obviously in Nubian. The Bari adjective has to be marked for number and gender *lo* masculine and *na* feminine which corresponds to the Maasai *ole,* fem *eng*. Many Bari nouns have the prefix /-k/ which they claim correspond to the cognate Maasai feminine variant article *eng*:

Bari	*Maasai*	*Meaning*
k-omoŋ	eng-omom	face
-amulak	eng-amulak	saliva
k-upir-öt	eng-opir	hair/feather
k-ula	eng-kula	unrine

A similar *k/g* prefix is found in many Nubian languages though it is omitted from corresponding roots in Nilotic. It would therefore appear to be the case that Nubian and Bari once possessed feminine and perhaps masculine articles.

G'alat or alat	'adze (Nubian)
G'ugme or ugum	'owl' (Nubian)
Ogomu-t	owl (Dinka)
K'obosh	'shell' (Nubian)
Awoch	'shell' (Shilluk)
K'orab	'spider/wasp' (Nubian)
Orap	'spider/wasp' (Shilluk)

Numerals

Reconstructed Forms

Bari	Shilluk	Dinka	Nuer	Nubian	English
ker	a-kyel	tok	kel	guer	six
uryö	a-rio	rou	rau	orw	seven
dök	a-dak	dyak	diak	tyok	eight
uŋwan	aŋuen	aŋuan	ouan	–	four

There is a near similarity in the counting system from six to nine (6–9) in many of the Nilotic languages, including Nubian. Bari has two forms though, the old and the new numerals:

Old	*New*	*Gloss*
tu	geleŋ	one
öri	murek	two
sala	musala	three
uŋwan	iŋwan	four
kanat	mukanat	five
bu-kyer	bu-kyer	six
bu-ryo	bu-ryo	seven
bu-dök	bu-dök	eight
bu-ŋwan	bu-ŋwan	nine
mere	pwök	ten

Ker, uryo, dök and iŋwan may be assumed to approximate to the older forms: uŋuan 'four' in Maasai, Dinka, Shilluk, Nuer and other Nilotic languages. Nubian proximate counterparts are shown under the list of numerals above. Murray and Roy suggest that the numeral systems have a common origin. The Bari *mere* 'ten' is the same as the Nubian *bure* 'ten' in the Nubian dialect of Jabel Daier in Khordofan.

There are also resemblances in many **particles** common to both Bari and Nubian.

The copula

The copula in both languages is the morpheme /a/ 'is'. This morpheme is prefixed onto the verb in Bari while it is suffixed onto the verb in Nubian.

> Bari: Ɖun a-duma 'God is great'
> Nubian: ashri-an 'the girl is beautiful

G.W. Murray (1920) ascribes the plural suffixes, some of the verbal derivatives affixes, and the gender system and other complex morphological features to an alleged Hamito-Semitic influence.

Now the linguistic items that these authors cite as evidence of borrowing from Hamitic are in fact, inconsistent with the reason why and what one language borrows from another, and types linguistic elements languages borrow from one another but (see Swadesh; and others).

Consider the following forms (Table 4), from Bari and various Nubian dialects which, according to Murray and Roy, are evidence of borrowing by these languages from a Hamitic source:[20]

Perusing these forms, one can easily see that the data do not support Murray and Roy (1920) claim that these linguistic forms are loans from Hamitic. The forms listed in Table 4 are exactly the basic sort of vocabulary that no language would need to borrow from another. As a rule, languages only borrow lexical forms for cultural artifacts and concepts, which they do not themselves possess. The fundamental vocabulary in the list claimed to be evidence of borrowing is so common that, ignoring the phonological changes in the forms, it is evident that these forms have the same meanings. Fundamental vocabulary is just the sort of thing that languages do not borrow.

Table 4: *Roots common to Nubian and Bari*

Nubian	Dialect	Bari	English
kuru	KM	gure	palm dove
mâg	KD	mok	steal/ catch
mogor antelope	KD	mekor	buffalo
môn	KDM	man	hate
mule	KM	mere	mountain
ner	KD	nyar	desire/love
ô	KD	yo-yu	sing
ony	M	won	weep/leak
ôw		öri	two
tach tan	KM	teŋ	until
tan-ch	M	'daŋ	taste/lick
tog	KDM	tok	strike/break/cut
tuk	K	tok	peck, bite
turu	Dai	tuli	water pot
Ulut (charcoal)	K	pulöt	burning charcoal
wal	M	walala	boil/to be cooked
oura (scribe)	O.N.	wur	write
angi	M	'baK	enclosure
bog	KD	'buk	pour
bott	KD	'böt	flay/to skin
bugbuge (barren salty ground)	K	bugi	to become mouldy
bai	D	'bain	absent
aru (rain)	KD	ru	to water

deg (cover)	DM	**(lo) 'dek**	roof
deny	KM	**'diŋga**	to have intercourse with
desi (green)	KDM	**'deti**	green vegetable
Dilig (full of holes)	K	**dili**	hole
dog (sit on, ride)	M	**'dogu**	carry
Dôny M(educate)	M	**den**	to know, understand
dûr (reach)	K	**'dur**	arrive
duk	KDM	**'dok**	to carry, raise
dumm (seize)	M	**'dum**	to seize, get
cri	KDM	**karin**	name
ew	KD	**we**	to sow
gind	M	**gin**	to tear
jakum,	KM	**nyekum**	jaw
jawwar,	M	**ja'bwe**	rainy season
jer, (watercourse)	K	**jor**	pond
kina, (closet, privy)	M	**kin**	to close
kob, (shut)	KD (shut)	**koba**	to patch
korr,	KD	**gor**	to snore
kure	Dai	**kare**	river
kor-j, (break, split)	KM	**kor**	divide, share
kondo-n,	M	**kodoŋe**	left hand

Abbreviations: D. Dongolla: D, Dai; K, Kenus ; M, Mahas; O.N, Old Nubian.

Source: Morrey and Roy (1920)

That being the case, it is highly suspect that these lexical items are actually loans from Hamitic. A very likely possibility is that these words are not Hamitic but actually original Nubian and Bari words. If, however, it is indeed the case that the linguistic forms were loans from Hamitic to Bari and Nubian, then one would have to conclude that (a), either both Nubian and Bari were Hamitic or, (b) that Hamitic was a Nilotic language, if, indeed, it ever existed. But since it has been proven that no such language as Hamitic spoken by a people know as 'Hamites' ever existed (Greenberg 1950), we surmise that what were originally known as Nilo-Hamites, were, in fact, nothing but Nilotes.

Nevertheless, let us, for the sake of intellectual curiosity pursue the whole idea of a 'Hamitic existence.

Hamites: myth or reality

The term "Hamite" has been over-emphasized in the classification of the Black people living along the Nile Valley and their brethren living outside the Nile Valley. It is therefore extremely important that one understands the meaning and the etymology of this word. Fortunately, the word 'Hamite' has been in use since Biblical times.

The first time we hear of the word *Ham* is in the Genesis in the Bible. According to the Bible, Mesraim designates Egypt, and Canaan, the entire coast of Palestine and Phoenicia for the people of Near East. Sennar represents the Nubia Kingdom, the site where Nimrod left for Western Asia. Nearly all ancient historians agree that the inhabitants of the Nile Valley belonged to an African race-Negro, which first settled in Ethiopia on the Middle Nile. As summed up by Gaston Maspero (1846–1916), "By the almost unanimous testimony of ancient historians, they belonged to an African race which settled in Ethiopia, on the Middle Nile; 'following the course of the river, they gradually reached the sea". Moreover, the Bible states that Mesraim, son of Ham, brother of Cush (Kush), the Ethiopian, and of Canaan, came from Mesopotamia to settle with his children on the banks of the Nile' (Diop 1974:2).

According to the Bible, Egypt was populated by the offspring of Ham, (*sic Hamites*) ancestor of the Blacks. The descendants of Ham are Cush, Mesraim, Phut and Canaan. The descendants of Cush are Saba, Hevilla, Sabatha, Regma, and Sabathacha...Cush was the father of Nemrod; he was the first to conqueror the earth...Mesraim became the father of Ludim, Anamim, Laabim,

Nepthuhim, Phethrusim, Chasluhim...Canaan became the father of Sid, his first born, and Heth.

In the past, the Egyptians called their country *Kemit,* which means "black" in their language. Eisee Rechus (1882) suggested that the term K and, Kham (and Hamite) as used to refer to African people in the Genesis was how ancient Egyptians refer to their country. They called it Kernet and the Kalenjin word for country is emeet. The Pokot have retained the original Hem for notion. The Hebrews, however, corrupted the word and it came to mean heat, black or burned in their language. To corroborate the Bible story, Herodotus, the father of history, also confirmed that inhabitants of ancient Egypt were black in color. If that is indeed true, then by what magic wand did the children of Ham who were black, turn from black to white so that there are now 'white Hamites' as is implied in the classification above? According to Diop (1974), the whole history of Egypt, 'mixture of the early population with white nomadic elements, conquerors or merchants, became increasingly important as the end of the Egyptian period approached'. This was supported by Cornelius de Pauw who points out that:

> "...In the low epoch Egypt was almost saturated with foreign white colonies: Arabs in Coptos, Libyans on the future site of Alexandria, Jews around the city of Hercules (Avais?), Babylonians (or Persians) below Memphis, "fugitive Trojans" in the area of the great stone quarries east of the Nile, Carians and Ionians over by the Pelusiac branch" (see Diop 1974:5).

This enclave of white foreigners was accorded a chance to grab power when Psammetichus, the Egyptian king of the seventh century, unwittingly entrusted the defense of the kingdom to a treacherous troop of Greek mercenaries. As Diop notes, "An enormous mistake of Pharaoh Psammentichus was to commit the defense of Egypt to foreign troops and to introduce various colonies made up of dregs of the nations" (Diop 1974:5). The process of assimilation and the whitening of Egypt were intensified under the conquest of Alexander the Great. After the conquest of Egypt and under the Ptolemies, crossbreeding between the Greeks and black Egyptians flourished due to a policy of assimilation. "Nowhere was

Dionysus more favored, nowhere was he worshipped more adoringly and more elaborately than by the Ptolemies, who recognized his cult as an especially effective means of promoting the assimilation of the conquering Greeks and their fusion with the native Egyptians."[21]

The Biblical curse of the "tall black people who live along the Nile Valley' (Isaiah 18) is also evidence that the people who lived along the Nile Valley were originally black. The alleged curse by God on the black race was a concoction by the Jews to extract a hurt which they thought was visited on them by the blacks while they were captives in their country.

Diop (1974:5) gives some Biblical background to the origins of the curse. To determine the worth of Biblical evidence, he argues that we must examine the genesis of the Jewish people. 'How did they create the Bible in which the descendants of Ham, ancestors of Negroes and Egyptians would thus become accursed; what were the historical reasons for that curse'? Jewish history shows that those who would become the Jews entered Egypt numbering 70 rough, 'fearful shepherds, chased from Palestine by famine and attracted by that earthly paradise, the Nile Valley'.

These nomads were first warmly welcomed and according to the Bible, settled in the land of Goshen and became shepherds of Pharaoh's flock. Overtime, however, and as the population of the Jews increased, the Egyptians became apprehensive about the growing population of possible hostile alliances within its borders between the Jews and other hostile forces and became concerned. This concern developed into active hostility towards the Jews. As hostility grew, the conditions of the Jews became more and more difficult. The Bible says that they were made to work in construction work, serving as labourers in building the city of Ramses. For fear of an uprising, the Egyptians took rather extreme steps to reduce the population of the Jews by limiting their births and killing off male babies. The idea was to prevent this prolific minority from developing into a sizeable group that might pose a threat to the nation, or more likely, in time of war, join and 'increase enemy ranks'. This was the genesis of the persecutions of the Jewish people and was to remain marked for the rest of its history.

From now on, the Jewish minority 'withdrew within itself, would become Messianic by suffering and humiliation. Such moral terrain of wretchedness and hope favored the birth and development of religious sentiment'.

> "The circumstances were the more favorable because this race of shepherds, without industry or social organization (the only social cell was the patriarchal family), armed with nothing but sticks, could envisage no positive reaction to the technical superiority of the Egyptian people. It was to meet this crisis that Moses appeared, the first of the Jewish prophet, who, after minutely working out the history of the Jewish people from its origins, presented it in retrospect under a religious perspective. Thus he caused Abraham to say many things that the latter could not possibly have foreseen: for example the 400 years in Egypt" (Diop 1974:6).

In the light of this discussion, the debate on the purported classification of African languages, and whether or not, for example, some Nilotes are Hamites or some Hamites are Nilotes or all Nilotes are non-Hamites is really a debate on non-issues. It is a mere play on words, a strategy meant to befuddle the unwary. 'It is impossible to link the notion of Hamites, as we labored to understand it in official textbooks, with the slightest historical, geographical, linguistic, or ethnic reality. No specialist is able to pinpoint the birthplace of the Hamites (scientifically speaking), the language they spoke, the migratory route they followed, the countries they settled, or the form of civilization they may have left.[22] On the contrary, all the experts agree that this term has no serious content, and yet not one of them fails to use it as a kind of master key to explain the slightest evidence of civilization in Black Africa.

Current status of Nilotic languages

The argument whether there were Hamites and whether some Nilotes were Hamites, Semites, or Caucasians is no longer an issue, although there are still some scholars who want to maintain the old classification (see Vossen 1983:177–204; Dimmandaal 1983:239–270).

The current position is that there is only one large language family called Nilotic, divided into three subfamilies namely: (a) Western, (b) Eastern and (c) Southern Nilotic. The Western Nilotic branch is composed of the original Nilotic (Dinka, Nuer, Shilluk, Acholi, Dholuo, Anuak and others. The so called Nilo-Hamitic group was broken up into two sub-families, namely: Bari, Maasai, Lotuho, Teso, Karimojong, Toposa and others making up the Eastern branch, while the Kalenjin group (Nandi, Kiyo, Marakwet, Pokot and others) made up the southern branch.

One thing that should be pointed out from the outset is that the term "Nilotic", designating the people who live or lived along the Nile Valley in 'North-South direction' is still undefined. What did they call themselves before they were renamed by other people? Where along the Nile Valley did they live? Why are many of them found thousands of miles far away from the Nile Valley? What caused them to move? Could they have migrated there if they lived along the Nile? These intriguing questions demand for some answers.

In the next Chapter, we attempt to provide some answers for Bari only, although in doing so, it will be necessary to refer to other related groups.

4

Bari in Pre-History

It is impossible to recover the pre-history of the Bari people without relating it to the history of other related groups. If we have gone into great length in discussing philosophical and methodological issues involved in the classification of African languages, it is only because we feel these issues would shed some light into the understanding of how people were classified into purported linguistic, racial, and cultural niches. We particularly believe that this may help clarify the controversy surrounding the linguistic, cultural and racial affiliation of the Bari people.

What happened in the very distant past is beyond the pale of memory of an individual or the collective memories of the community as whole. Most of that history is buried deep in the sands of history and may only be accessed indirectly, through some of the techniques alluded to earlier.

We have seen from the various classifications that Bari belongs to the Nilotic family of languages. The question that arises is how did it become so different, in fact, so different as to be mistaken for a different language, if indeed it was different at all? When and why did it diverge, if it did, from the rest of the group? The Africanist historian Ehrets (1971) suggests some plausible answers to the questions. He observes that:[23]

> "A people's history does not begin with their memories. It begins rather with their emergence as a separate group. If their emergence and early development lie beyond the reach of the historian's familiar source, human memory as it appears in documents and oral traditions, the historian cannot therefore say that such events are darkness and not history" (Ehret 1971).

Such a history, he continues, would be a different sort of history; it would be a history without heroes, or dated events relating to particular wars, but it would nonetheless be history. The historian should legitimately utilize whatever sources he can to penetrate the darkness and reveal it as history. The history of the Bari people in the period before 1200 AD must be this kind of history.

In reconstructing the history of eras for which there are neither documentary sources nor oral tradition, linguistic evidence holds much the same position that documentary evidence holds in the reconstruction of histories of literate periods. Using linguistic evidence and techniques, the basic structure of the history can be rebuilt. Taken together with linguistic data drawn from other Nilotic languages, a broad picture of the undocumented portion of the history can be reconstructed. Reconstruction assumes a common genetic relationship of languages. As we have already explained, genetic relationship implies the existence of a common ancestor language known as a proto-language from which all the other related languages descended. The more distant in space and time the relationship between the languages, the earlier in time the proto-language was spoken.

With greater time depth, a proto-language may break up into a series of subsequent proto-languages, much like what happened to old Latin, giving rise to: Italian, French, Spanish, Portuguese and Catalan. Each proto-language requires the past existence of a community speaking that language. That way, a sequence of communities existing at various times in the past can be set up. The earliest community is that which spoke the proto-language, in our particular case, proto-Nilotic.

That being the case, we can assume that the Nilotes were once one people who spoke one language, proto-Nilotic, before they broke up into smaller groups. We further conjecture that in addition to speaking the same language, they must have lived in one geographical place and shared a common culture.

A break in the proto-language constitutes a node. A node marks a time sequence in the break up between proto-languages. It therefore marks the beginning of divergence between languages and communities. The community at each nodal period would not necessarily have been a united people speaking a language without dialects. The norm would be that there would a cluster of several very closely associated peoples speaking closely related dialects of the proto-language. As is natural process with human languages, the proto-language would be gradually undergoing change, in vocabulary, phonology and eventually grammatical structure. Change would be minimal if the people speaking the same language live together within a small area and remain in constant communication with each other.

Changes appearing in one of the dialects would not be localized to one dialect, but shared by all of them. Since changes would affect the whole of the dialects, there would be change but the language would still remain as one language. But if communication between the speakers of dialects of one language were blocked or interrupted by wide distances or by physical or other barriers, the change may be such that communication may well break down. Subsequent changes occurring in the various dialects become localized and affect only a specific dialect found in a specific area. New dialectal differences would appear and old ones would grow greater in different parts of the country. The continuation of this process would mark the breakup of the nodal community and of the proto-language spoken in it. If the separation between the dialects persisted, eventually the differences would be so great that the former dialects of the proto-language would become separate languages; no longer mutually intelligible. At this point, a new language or languages are born.

Let us return to and hypothesize about what happened to the Nilotic peoples. As we intimated above, these people, who spoke one language, lived in the same area and shared a common culture, began to breakup for a variety of reasons, causes that we will look at later on. It would seem that the Proto-Nilotic broke up into three daughter proto-languages; namely: (a) proto-Western Nilotic, the ancestor of the present Western Nilotes (Dinka, Nuer, Shilluk, Acholi, etc), (b), proto-Eastern Nilotic, the mother of the Eastern Nilotic group of languages (Bari, Maasai, Lotuho, Teso, Toposa, etc) and (c) proto-Southern, the precursor of the Kalenjin group of languages (Nandi, Kipsigis, Keyo, etc.).[24]

Since our interest is in Bari and Bari is classified as belonging to Eastern-Nilotic branch of Nilotic, now let us look at what happened to this branch in some detail.

Eastern Nilotic history begins with the development of a separate Eastern Nilotic speech out of one of the dialects of proto-Nilotic (Diagram 1). From available linguistic data, (Rottland 1982; Vossen 1982; Espangolo 1933; Tucker and Bryan 1963; Greenberg 1953), Proto-Eastern Nilotic consisted of Bari, Lotuho, Teso, Turkana and Maasai. Overtime subsequent splits occurred.

Diagram 1: *Proto-Nilotic dialects*

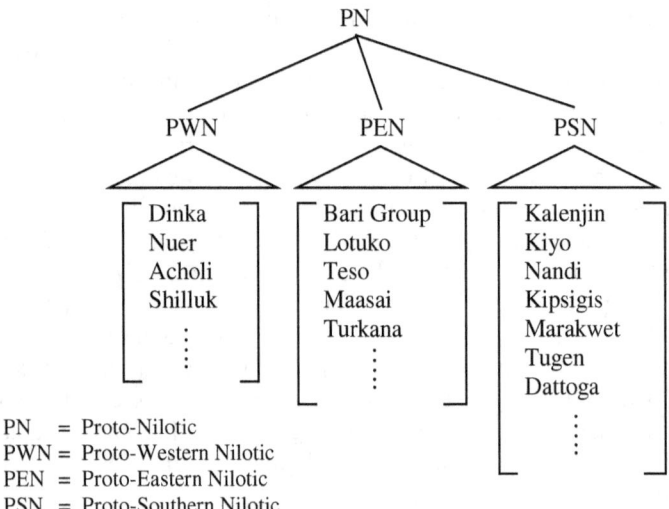

PN = Proto-Nilotic
PWN = Proto-Western Nilotic
PEN = Proto-Eastern Nilotic
PSN = Proto-Southern Nilotic

This classification was arrived at by applying three methods (Diagram 2) in establishing relatedness between these languages groups, namely: "Swadesh classification", "Gleason classification", and "Genetic classification" (comparative method).

The Swadesh and Gleason (1959) methods are the "classical" approaches used for calculating "the characteristic vocabulary index". The methods consist in comparing 157 words from a list of carefully selected word-list of 200 items (but see Lehman 1963:112f: Vossen 1982:105f). These words are then compared in terms of meaning, word order, phonetic inventory and phonological processes.

Diagram 2: *Three genetic classification methods*

(a) Swadesh classification

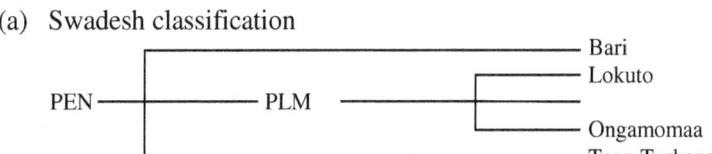

(b) Gleason classification

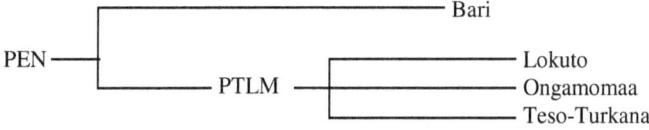

(c) Genetic classification (comparative method)

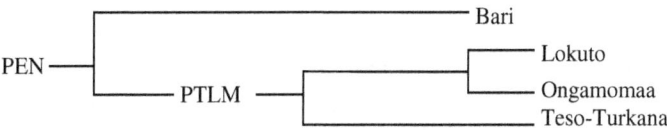

PWN = Proto-Eastern Nilotic
PTLM = Proto-Teso-Lokuto-Man
PLM = Proto-Lotuko-Man

Sources: Vossen, (1982), p: 185

On the bases of these methods, four units of closely related languages are established namely: (a) Bari (b) *Lotuko* (c) *Teso-Turkana* (d) *Ongamo-Maa*. The "Gleason approach"—really a comparative method—shows that there are two primary branches of Eastern Nilotic, namely; Bari and Non-Bari. However, it should be noted that the three methods give mixed results concerning secondary branches. Implicitly, however, the classifications suggest that there are at least three proto-stages of splits in agreement with the proposal put forward by Ehret (1971). The three proto-stages are: (a) Proto-Eastern Nilotic (b) Proto-*Teso-Lotuko-Maa* and (c) Proto-*Lotuko-Maa*. We shall not go into the technical details of how the comparative method works in practice. Here, it suffices to say that Bari is closely related to these languages. In spite of the mixed results, it is, nevertheless, possible to delineate about at least five secondary nodal communities, representing six proto-splits since the break up of Eastern-Nilotic. These are: (1) the proto-Eastern Nilotic period, (2) the Proto-Bari period (made of up *Bari, Kuku, Kakwa, Nyangwara, Fajulu and Mundari*) (3), the proto-*Lotuho-Turkana-Toposa-Teso-Maasai* period, (4) the proto-*Lotuho-Turkana* period, and (5), the proto-*Teso-Maasai* period.

Thus, the first primary split of Proto-Eastern Nilotic was into Bari and non-Bari groups (the groups other than Bari). Each of the two groups would represent a proto-stage of development. We would, therefore, have proto-Bari and proto-Lotuho-Teso-Turkana-Maasai. The Bari group consisted of the present six dialects of Bari, namely; *Bari, Mundari, Kakwa, Fajulu, Nyangwara* and *Kuku*.[25] This group has remained fossilized and has undergone little change, although, as is to be expected, there are discernible dialectal differences.

The non-Bari group underwent further split; first, into proto-Lotuho-Turkana-Toposa and then into proto-Teso-Maasai-Gram. Eventually, each of the languages in the proto-languages broke up into their ultimate parts. Again, we should recall that each of the point in the break constitutes a proto-stage in development.

It is important to note that since each of the splits represents a time span, languages within the same cluster in the split would tend to be more closely related and probably more intelligible than languages in a cluster further up in a different node. The further up the languages in the node, the older they are. Consequently, Bari would be considered as older than the other languages because it is the only language that has not undergone further fragmentation and it is further up the genealogical tree and has remained unchanged since the split of Eastern proto-Nilotic from proto-Nilotic.

Migration vs diffusion

Splits portend change. As we have seen, languages may change due to language internal dynamics or man induced causes such as separation of related peoples by great distances because of movement or prolonged separation. However, languages may also undergo change, not because of movement, but because of what is termed diffusion of linguistic features. Like the movement of water waves, a wave propagated from one end of a pond quickly travels to the other end without physical movement. It is alleged that linguistic and cultural changes may also happen in a similar manner.

In the literature, the two terms are often used synonymously. They are often adduced to account for a situation where similar cultures and languages spread over a wide geographical area like the one that obtains among the Nilotic languages. Both of these concepts assume that cultural resemblances are a consequence of historical connections originating from the movement of cultural features. All that one needs to assert, without contradiction, is that the observed linguistic, or cultural resemblances are due to nothing else, but the diffusion of these features from area A to B to C and so on. No movement is involved.

Thus, one can logically assert that the Nilotic languages and peoples from the Sudan to Tanzania and from Ethiopia to the Central Democratic Republic of the Congo share common cultural and linguistic resemblances, not because they have necessarily physically moved into these areas but because of the diffusion of these resemblances. We that the Nilotic people are dispersed over a large area of East and Central Africa, spread across six countries; namely: the Sudan; where most of them reside; Western Ethiopia; Uganda; Kenya; Tanzania and the Democratic Republic of the Congo. According to Spagnolo (1933:XVII):

"This zone presents a rough triangle whose eastern side starts from Kilimanjaro mountain and coasting the western banks of Lake Rudolf present Lake Turkana, reaches the southwest boundaries of Ethiopia from where the northern side begins and following a line almost parallel to the lat. 6° N, and goes so far as to graze the long. 20° E. The third side descends south-east and after partly coinciding with, and cutting, the north-east border of the Belgian Congo (present Democratic Republic of the Congo), enters Uganda (West Nile District) and, turning eastwards, reaches Mount Elgon by an arc, whose convex points to the north-east. It then curves decidedly to the south, and following a very irregular line, closes the triangle at the great rocks of Kilimanjaro".

Proponents of this theory argue that what is needed for communities to share linguistic and cultural features is contiguity, not necessarily physical movement of populations. In this view, these languages share common features simply because their speakers have been in contact for an extended period of time. In a nutshell, it is the shared abstract features that have moved, not the people themselves. Thus, yes, Nubian, may share the same linguistic features with, Shilluk, or Maasai, but that does not necessarily mean that these groups once lived in the same area but moved away from one another over time. This view subtly denies the possibility of these groups from ever migrating from a common original geographical area.

However, assuming for the moment that the proponents of diffusionism are right, one wonders where these alleged shared features come from, for the features themselves presuppose the antecedent existence of a dominant donor language or culture before they can ever spread. Furthermore, the diffusion of these features requires the existence of a continuum of related communities and languages through which they spread. Features do not cross discontinuous groups. They just do not jump across truncated groups.

Take the linguistic relationship between Nubian, Bari and the Maasai and the great span of distance that separates the three communities. Nubian is found in southern Egypt and the extreme north of the northern Sudan; Bari is located near the extreme end of the Sudan in the southern Sudan; Maasai in the eastern and nearly southern part of Africa in Tanzania. If the common elements in these languages were due to diffusion or borrowing from a third, donor language alleged to have been Hamitic, where was this Hamitic language spoken before it mysteriously disappeared? As Murray and Roy pointed out, "At later period Hamito-Semitic influences permeated three of the groups, Nubian, Bari, and Maasai, which we therefore call Nilo-Hamitic, and to a slight extent, affected the Shiluk group also."[26] Of course, we now know that this was mere myth. No such language or a people who spoke Hamitic ever existed. While diffusion of linguistic features may account for some of the observed resemblances between Nilotic languages and cultures, it does not rule out the possibility of migration.

Migration of Nilotes

Diffusionism may have some explanatory plausibility in certain circumstances, but it cannot wholly explicate the pervasive incidences of close cultural and linguistic relationships between the Nilotic Diaspora. It is not only counterfactual, but it actually denies the possibility of these groups from ever having been in one area and then moved apart due to a variety of causes. Based on the parameters of simplicity and explanatory adequacy, migration would appear to be a more plausible theory. If that is indeed the case, and assuming that the Nilotic peoples had lived in one area and then moved away from each other, then the great resemblances in linguistic, cultural, and even physical features between them should not be surprising. There would be no good reason to posit the existence of non-existent donor language that 'disappeared without trace' to account for the similarities between the so-called "Nilo-Hamitic" languages and the so-called "Nilotic" languages proper. The observed similarities can simply be attributed to common origin, simple and pure. This would not only meet the standards of observational, but explanatory adequacy (Chomsky 1957).

Now a plethora of evidence exist which point to the fact that the home of the Nilotes was in the Nile Basin, or in the Sahara east of the Nile Basin before the Sahara dried up around 7000 BC (Herodotus 1954; Ibin Batuta 1843; Ibin Khaldun, 1954, and Strabo) to mention but a few.

Movement of people out of the Nile Valley started many millenniums ago and mainly from two principal causes: the desiccation of the Sahara and the relentless incursions of Asiatic hordes into the Nile Basin. For 5000 years, before it began to dry up, the region now covered by Sahara was once teeming with life. It was a land of lakes, rivers, forests, green fields, farms, villages, towns and cities. Wild life was in plenty. Around 7000 BC, however, the Sahara began to dry up slowly, forcing the inhabitants to move in equally small waves away from the encroaching desert. Overtime, this developed into an exodus. Coupled with this cataclysmic climatic change of the region was then added ever present pressures from all manner of invading hordes of whites from the earliest times: Canaanites, Hebrews, Phoenicians, Mongols, Arabs, Berbers, Greeks, Romans and so on. All these pressures led to an exodus of the blacks from their ancestral lands to the east, west, and south and into the interior of the continent, a continent that generally until the exodus, was inhabited by a race of small people and pygmies (Herodotus).[27]

The migrations were of many different kinds (Williams, 1976). There was no general flight of people, here and there all over the continent. Rather the movements were slow and sporadic. There were groups that moved only a relatively short distance each time, and as a whole never left the general area. These movements may rightly be termed migration eddies—circular movements within the same geographical area. Even where the groups had migrated furthest, the movement was slow, and often forced by circumstances beyond the control of the local community—inexorable adverse climatic change and the indefatigable enemies of the blacks, the hordes of white invaders.

In this general atmosphere of uncertainty and extreme inhospitality, the Nilotes left their ancestral home in all directions. They fled to the west, following the edges of the Sahara to the Atlantic Ocean; to the southwest into the Congo tropical forests; south into the sudds of southern Sudan, and east along the Red Sea and along the coast of the Indian Ocean and into the Ethiopian highlands.

The Western Nilotes dispersed in two main directions: west towards the Atlantic Ocean, and south, west and east along the Nile into the sudds in the Bahr el Ghazal and Upper Nile regions of southern Sudan. The bulk remained in the swamps or areas surrounding the swamps, where they grazed their cattle and remained protected from their implacable enemies until modern time. This constitutes the bulk of the western Nilotic group the Dinka, Nuer, Shilluk, and the Anuak. Other groups got out of the swamps and moved over land on both sides of the Nile into the present day East Africa and the Ethiopian highlands. The Dholuo, Anuak, the Acholi, and the rest of the Luo group belong to this later category.

The Eastern and Southern Nilotes; namely: the Bari, Lotuho, Teso, Maasai, Toposa, Kamojong, Nandi, Tugens, Kiye, Marakwets and so on, tracked to the east and along the Red Sea coast into the Ethiopian Highlands. Somewhere along the way, the two groups parted ways.[28] The Eastern Nilotes veered from the Ethiopian Highlands towards the Nile, just a little south of the sudd and continued moving southward up to Lake Rudolf (Lake Turkana) and to the west and south of Lake Victoria. The Bari belongs to this later group.

After separation from the eastern Nilotes, the southern Nilotes continued their movement in a southerly direction, east of the Nile and west of the Indian Ocean to approximately their present locations. As pointed out earlier, this movement took place over a long period, allowing time for cultural, linguistic and other changes to take place along the way.[29]

The model being proposed here is that instead of (PN) splitting up simultaneously into three groups, the first split is into two primary groups; namely, Proto-Western (PWN) and proto-none Western Nilotic groups (NPWN) (see Diagram 3). The (NPWN) originally known as Nilo-Hamites, then underwent further separation into Proto-Eastern Nilotic (PEN) and proto-Southern Nilotic (PSN) *(See diagrams 1, 2 and 3).*

Diagram 3: *Two primary genetic groups*

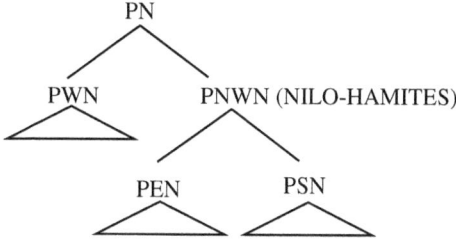

5

Bari Migration

What were the movements of the Bari people in these conundrums of mass migrations? No one knows precisely, but generally, the movement of the Bari people is part of the general exodus of the Nilotic peoples from their cradle in the Nile Basin. When they moved out of the Nile Basin and when they separated from the rest of the larger Nilotic group is a matter of conjecture. However, there is reason to believe that they are a part of a group that moved out of the Nile Basin and trekked eastwards towards the Red Sea area.

As alluded to above, the movement has been slow and over a long time, lasting thousand of years. The Bari are most probably a part of the many splinter groups that moved out of the Nile Valley in the long sea-saw battles that raged on over the millennia between the blacks and the invading Caucasians from across the Mediterranean and the Red Sea.

It is not easy to fix a date, but a probable time that spurred their movement out of the Nile Valley was before or after the collapse of the Nubian Kingdom when the 'Bhkat Treaty"—a stand-off between the Arab invaders and Nubia that lasted for one thousand years - came to an end in about 641 AD.[30] There are two reasons in support of this view. One, if the comparison of fundamental vocabulary is proof that Bari and Nubian are related, then the Bari must have originated from where the Nubians are now to be found. Two, the Bari pride themselves as being the masters of the bow, which they alleged, they inherited from their forefathers, who had always had the bow since time immemorial.

Now, ancient Nubia was famous for its skilful archers, who gallantly kept off invaders at bay from their land for considerable periods in history. Citing oral traditions, Spagnolo (1933), writes that the Bari consider the bow (*dang*) to be their original weapon of war. They pride themselves to be as a people with 'quiver, bow and arrows' (*dang, gwolo ko lowiya*) unlike the Beri "*yi a 'bari kogwon yi ko dang*; yi *'bayin ko 'bukwö så ko gwolo ti kala gwoso Böri*" (Spagnolo 1933*)*. Unlike the other Nilotes found in the area, such as the Lotuko and the Lokoya whose weapon of war was the spear, the Bari would seem to have acquired the spear at a later date.

The Bari considered themselves different from the rest of the people in the area. This is embodied in the Bari saying that "*yi a Bari*. Now, the meaning of the word '*Bari*' is uncertain. Spagnolo (1933) speculates that perhaps it was the same as the indefinite pronoun "*bari*", meaning someone else, as in the expression, "*Yi a bari*" (we are a people different from others). According to oral traditions recorded by Spagnolo, in the olden times, the Bari were also called Morsak, Dongoda or 'Yure. Indeed the first Europeans to come into contact with the Bari thought they were different from the people in the area. They were so impressed with their classical features that they compared them to "Roman aristocrats and Egyptian murals" (Verne 1841). Verne declared that the Bari might well constitute "the protoplasm of the black race". Lafargue, another European who visited the Bari in 1844, thought that the Bari were "the most beautiful human race that exists on earth". Hartmanns (1884:129) believed that "the Bari might very well provide us with a model of the authentic 'noble savage'. Similar assessments of their physique and health were common throughout the nineteenth century.

As to where they came from, the Bari themselves are not entirely certain, although there are legends recorded that are alleged to indicate from where they came. There are two main legends that attempt to explain from where the Bari migrated. One legend recorded in Spagnolo (1933:XII) says that the Bari came to the Nile Basin from the east, from around the shores of Lake Rudolf (Turkana). The other legend, noted in Haddon (1911), claims that the Bari came to the area they now live in from the East North East (E.N.E). Let us examine the merits of each of the legends, beginning with the one that states that the Bari came to their present home from the east.

Migration from the East

According to the Spagnolo (1933:XII) version,

> "The place and origin of the Bari is uncertain, and likewise what family they are, whether "Nilotic", or "Hamitic", or, rather, "Niloto-Hamitic". Local traditions claim that the Bari came originally from the eastern shore of Lake Rudolf. "All good things comes from the east; from the west, nothing may be hoped for", as they say. The "Rainmakers", also, used to turn themselves to the north-east, when they performed their ceremonies to obtain rain".

Other than the quote above, Spagnolo does not say anything more about the legend. Now let us take a moment to speculate freely about the legend. You will recall that we have hypothesized that the Bari were a part of the group that moved east from the Nile Basin towards the Red Sea. If that is indeed the case, how did they end up in the eastern shores of Lake Rudolf, now renamed 'Lake Turkana' as claimed by the legend. Did, in fact, the Bari specifically mention Rudolf or just some lake? Suppose that they meant some other lake other than Lake Rudolf and that Spagnolo (1933) substituted 'Lake Rudolf' for the lake mentioned in the legend. In any case, the lake did not bear the name of either 'Rudolf' or 'Turkana' because these names were given at later date. It would help matters if the native name for the lake were given. As things stand, it leaves the possibility open that the lake alluded to could have been any other lake not necessarily Lake Rudolf/Turkana. Logically, nothing prevents one from speculation that this 'lake' could have been just any other lake that happen to lie on their path of migration on their way to the Nile Basin.

In any event, if the Bari came from 'Lake Rudolf', it follows that they must have lived around the lake, in which case they would have had some name for it, or at least known what it was called by those who lived along the shores of the lake at the time. Could Spagnolo, in fact, have been mistaken in attributing a specific name to the lake the Bari left on their final leg to the Nile Basin? Now, suppose that the alleged Lake Rudolf in the legend was, in fact, Lake Tana.

Be it as it may, let us suppose, for the sake of argument that the legend was, in fact, correct that the Bari migrated to the Nile Valley from around the shores of Lake Turkana. The legend would seem to win credibility from the fact that, based on our classification, the communities of the primary split from proto-Nilotic are still to be found around the Lake Rudolf (Turkana) area, or near it. Groups such as Turkana, Toposa, Lotuho and Maasai, also claim that their original home was around the Lake Turkana area (Demandaal 1983; Tucker and Bryen 1963; Ehret 1972, and others). Nevertheless, it may still well be the case that the legend is, in fact, correct, but only to the extent that Lake Rudolf/Turkana was the final stage for the Bari to launch their final push to the Nile Basin after long and tedious journeys. Conceding that to be true, still that is not sufficient ground to conclude that the split between the Bari and the Non-Bari communities necessarily occurred around the shores of Lake Rudolf (Turkana).

The other difficulty with the claim made by the legend, unfortunately, often reinforced by Africanist historians - such Ehret (1971), Tucker and Bryen (1963), Greenberg (1953), Spagnolo (1933) and Muratori (1933)- runs contrary to the general thesis that the original homeland of the Nilotic peoples was in the north, further up in the Nile Valley. These writers are of the general opinion that the ancestral home of the Nilotes, especially the Eastern Nilotes was around the East African rift valley. They would not hear of these groups coming from any where but the rift valley.

If it is indeed true, as the legend alleges, that the original home of the Bari was around Lake Rudolf/Turkana area, then it should also be true that Lake Turkana/Rudolf was the homeland of all Nilotic peoples. Of course, we know this is absolute nonsense. It would not only go contrary to the established facts that the ancestral homeland of the Nilotic peoples was along the Nile Valley (Herodotus), but it would make it nearly impossible to explain cultural, linguistic and racial relatedness between Western, Eastern and Southern Nilotic peoples.

In any case, if indeed the Bari migrated to the Nile Basin from the east— from around the Lake Turkana area as claimed by Spagnolo (1933), Muratori (1933) and others - then one would also have to admit of the possibility of north-south migration. Many writers writing on the movement of the eastern Nilotic peoples insist on a south-north migration, not a north-south migration. They place the ancestral home of the Eastern Nilotes somewhere in East Africa, Ehret (1971), Tucker and Bryan (1963) and others. They do not accept the thesis that the original homeland of the Nilotic was further up in the Nile Valley. Some however concede, albeit grudgingly, that the Bahr el Ghazal area may be a probable ancestral home of the Nilotes, at least for the Western Nilotic peoples. The legend raises more questions than answers.

A further problem with the legend is, if indeed the Bari migrated into the Nile area from the east, from the shores of Lake Rudolf/Turkana, why was it only the Bari that came to the Nile Basin and not the others? Which route did they follow from the shores of Lake Turkana to the Nile area?

The Bari migrated from the North

Now let us consider the legend that the Bari migrated from the north to the site they now live in. According to Haddon (1911:468), quoting from the missionary Morlang (182/3:117), the Bari claim that their ancestors came to the area they now occupy from the north. The legend claims that long ago, the Bari and the Berri were once one tribe living 50 miles East, North East of Gondokoro. During the reign of one Tombe of the Nyori clan, a quarrel arose between some of his followers and those of another chief as to "whether a certain woman who was *enceine* (sic pregnant) would give birth to twins or a single infant." Being in a hurry to resolve the issue, the woman was killed before she could go to full term.

Instead of settling the matter, a quarrel ensued that resulted in war between the two groups. Since neither group defeated the other, it was agreed that a further waste of life was unnecessary; "that Tombe and his people and one half of the Bari-Berri clan and rainstones, should go to the East, and the other portion should remain where they were". That was why Tombe of the Nyori clan came to the Nile Valley and that was the reason why the Bari came to live along the Nile. Tombe became the progenitor of the Bari and the other unnamed chief the ancestor of the Berri. Was there indeed a Bari-Berri split?

Let us see whether we can make sense of this legend. Let us begin with the assumed relation between the Bari and the Berri. You will recall that in our genetic reconstruction of Nilotic languages, Proto-Nilotic communities first split into two daughter families, namely: Proto-Western Nilotic and proto-non-Western Nilotic. The Non-Proto-Western Nilotic group underwent further split and broke up into Proto-Eastern Nilotic and Proto-Southern Nilotic. The communities that made up proto-Western Nilotic were Dinka, Nuer, Anuak, Shilluk, Acholi, Dholuo, Japhadola, Alur, Pari, Jur-Bel and others. The groups that made up the non-proto-Western family were Bari, Lotuho, Masaai, Turkana, Teso, Toposa, Jei, Logir, Lakoya, Nandi, Tugen, Keiyo, Marakwet and so on. This latter group was what was called the 'Nilo-Hamites'. When it broke up, one group was called Eastern Nilotic composed of the Lutuho, Bari, Masaai, Teso, Turkana, Toposa, and Karimojong and so on. The rest of the group belonged to the Southern Nilotic Branch, now renamed as the Kalenjin.

Proto-Eastern Nilotic, which is the focus of our discussion, separated into Bari and non-Bari groups. The Non-Bari groups are all the languages of the eastern Nilotic branch (Lotuho, Teso, Toposa, Turkana, Karimojong, Maasai and others), other than of course, Bari. The Bari group remains the six dialects of Bari; namely: Bari, Kakwa, Fajulu, Mundari, Nyangwara and Kuku. If there were a split, then, Tombe would have to be the chief of the Bari group and the other unnamed chief, the chief of the Non-Bari section, i.e. of Lotuho, Teso and so on.

That is implausible, however. Recall that in our genetic classification, Berri belongs to the Southern-Western Nilotic family and is closer to Acholi and Shilluk than to either Bari or Lotuho. It therefore, cannot, be possible that the Bari separated from Berri as suggested by the legend. It is however possible that the *Bari* and the *Berri* might have crossed paths in their endless cycles of migrations in their quest for new settlements.

Another thing, which is not clear from the legend, is whether the word intended is indeed Berri or Pari. The two words are homophonous. It is important to know which name is meant because while there is indeed a tribe known as Pari, the Bari of southern Bari and the Lotuho refer to the Acholi who are their neighbours as Böri and Vari respectively. The Bari also refer to Pari as Böri lo-koro to differentiate them from Böri—Acholi. If it is Pari that is intended in the legend then there could not have been a split between Bari and Pari for the reasons given above. The two belong to two different nodal communities. If there is any relation at all, it is because they originated from a common ancestor—proto-Nilotic. Pari is far more closely related to Acholi than it is to Bari.

There are those who believe that the legend is actually true. They argue that the word Bari could have actually been Pari. If Tombe the chief of the Bari who brought them to the Nile Basin was a Berri/Pari, then the Bari must have been Paris. How else could the chief of the Pari suddenly become the chief of the Bari if he was not himself a Bari, or the Berri and the Bari were not the same people? If that is true, then one is left with no option but to draw the conclusion that the Bari must have been essentially Luos! The fact that the Nyori clan to which chief Tombe belongs is one of the largest and the oldest rain making clan amongst the Bari, supports this conclusion. It predates the Bekat. This clan is also a prominent clan among the Pari. Before the coming of the Nyori clan, the Bari had no rainmakers. The most prominent person was the *monyekak* (the land chief), or *monyelori* (the chief of the pointed spear). We examine the relations between the moneykak and the matat-lo-pioŋ in subsequent chapters. The important question, however, is, how did the Luos become Bari, if the legend is true? Were there existing Bari tribes that then assimilated chief Tombe and his group, or did the Luo language just change irrevocably?

So much for the composition of the Bari tribe. Let us now consider their line of movement. According to the legend, the Bari say they came from a place about 50 miles E.N.E. of Gondokoro. That will take us past the Badingilo plains to Lafon hills. Indeed, there is alleged to be a remnant of a Bari speaking tribe around the *Lotuke* area at *Lafon.* The *Jei* people who live in the area say that some of their relatives left them and went east after a quarrel caused by the sharing of soup. The parting took place under the foot of a mountain that at a distance looked blue at the top and grey at the bottom. It had zebra marks and was therefore named *lótúké*. Now, */tókè/*, in Bari stands for the mixture of the colours black, blue and grey. */lo/* is merely a masculine gender marker, for in Bari, a noun must be either masculine or feminine.

Now, how did the group that came towards the Nile become a mixture of the Jei and the Pari? Could these have been the constituent groups that would eventually make up the Bari tribe? It is not at all obvious that that was the case, but it would seem that a lot of work still needs to be done to answer these questions.

Let us suppose that the movement towards the Nile started from the N.E., instead of E.N.E. as suggested by the legend. That will land us in the Lake Tana area in southwestern Ethiopia. If that were the case, their migratory path to Gondokoro would have to be in a southwesterly direction.

Now from around the Lake Tana area the group would have to go southeast into the Lofon hills where this Jei-Bari split would have occurred. The Bari would veer west towards the Nile and would settle around the Bor area, slightly northwards from where they now are, not Gondokoro, which is further to the south. This would be consistent with the view that the Bari merely came from the east, but their previous homeland was in the north. In this view, although their long sojourn ended up in the south, it was necessary for them to take zigzag paths for a variety of reasons; to avoid hostile enemies, uninhabitable terrains such as deserts, mosquito-infested swamps and mountain ranges.

It is possible that foreigners recording Bari oral traditions mistook Lake Tana for Lake Rudolf (now Lake Turkana) when the Bari say that they came from the east from the shores of some lake. It is probable that based on the similarity of ethnic composition of the communities surrounding Lake Turkana with the Bari, writers like Spagnolo (1963; XI) surmised that the Bari must have also originated from around that area.

Further support for the north-south migration hypothesis comes from place names. Place names are reliable indicators for early settlement. In the absence of any archeological evidence to support the claim for early settlement, names are also usually, for historical record, taken to be reliable indicators for early presence.

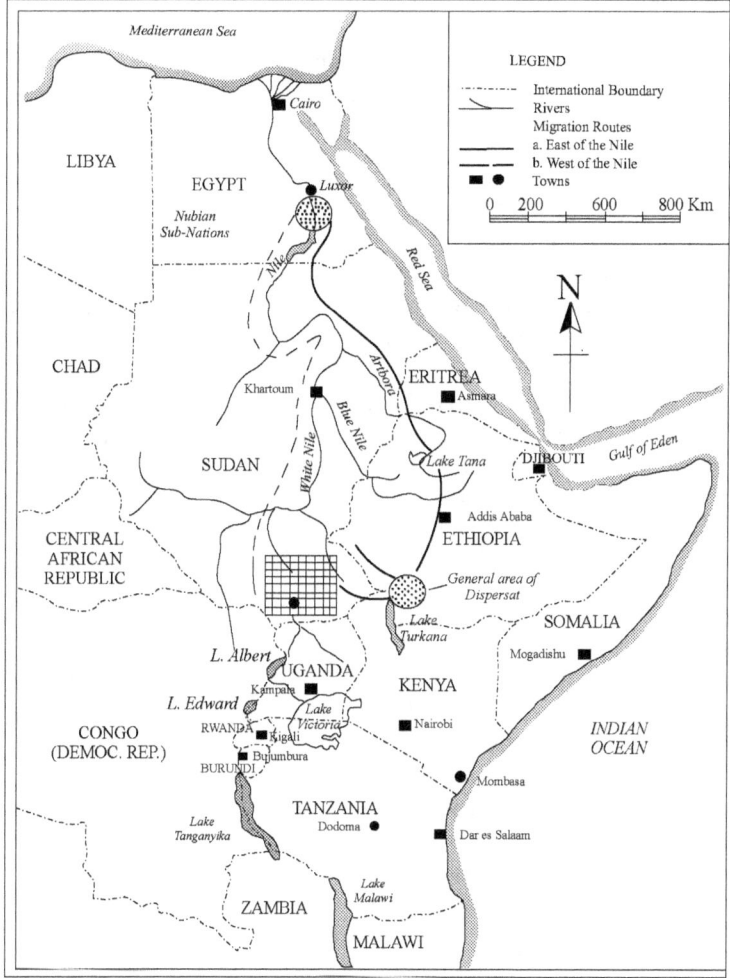

Figure 1: *Geographical location of the Bari-speaking peoples and possible route of migration.*

Such evidence exists for the claim that the Bari first settled around the Bor area, or in fact, further north because there are place names that bear unmistakable Bari names. Take the name Bor, for example. 'Bor', is actually 'bar' in Bari and has the same meaning in both languages–'flood'. Other place names are: *'kare lo Wani'*, the river of Wani); *'kol marek'* (actually *kolong murek*), (two suns); *Jale*, (name); *dorkolong, 'doro na kolong*, (sunset); *pan-Modi,* (the home of Mödi), also found in the Bor area. Now Bor is immediately to the north of the Bari.

Before the Dinka Bor moved east across the Nile from Baher el Ghazel, Bor area was inhabited by the Bari before they moved south due to constant flooding. These are just a few examples that appear to support the possibility of earlier occupancy of the Bor area by the Bari and are consistent with a theory of north-south migration of the Bari. The eastern theory of migration is observationally correct but it should not be used to make the unwarranted conclusion that the ancestral home of the Bari was in the east—the shores of Lake Rudolf.

Actually, one might assume that the migration started further north, south of present day Egypt. We have actually already made the north-south migration claim. We have hypothesized that the Bari and kindred groups moved out of the Nile Basin and moved to the east into the Red Sea area and into present day Eritrea. In fact, in Eritrea today, there are still remnants of these people who say that the greater part of their population had moved away from the area, leaving only a few of them behind. The people until recently still call themselves *Bari-ya*.[31] The *'ya'* comes from Arabic. There is also a place in Eritrea called *Bar-un-to*. The root of this word is ' bar' which in Bari means 'to bring' or 'take' something for somebody'. /un/ is bound morpheme and can function as an inchoative, or an adverbial suffix. As an adverbial suffix, it means to do something towards the speaker. The meaning of the bound morpheme /-to/ is also functionally determined. It could play a reflexive or causative role when pre-fixed or suffixed onto the verb. In this particular usage, it means together. Thus *"bar-u(n)-to"* in Bari means, 'to bring together'. The word therefore means 'bring them along', or 'those who came together'. This word has retained pretty much the same meaning even in Ethiopia today.

The Bari-speakers: myth or reality

From the time the Bari 'speaking peoples' moved into the Nile Basin, they are clustered together in a linguistic 'pocket' in the south and southwest of what used to be called 'Mongolla Province' extending from latitude 6° 5´ down to latitude 3° 5´ (see map), on both sides of the Nile, and having a maximum breadth of about 90 miles. Strictly speaking, the Bari are the main part of these Bari-speaking tribes, Spagnolo (1933:XII), and this is what are going to talk about here.

Is the word "Bari" what the Bari people used to call themselves? Contemporary Bari are not sure, but there are good grounds for believing that the word "Bari" was the original name the Bari used to refer to themselves. As we have seen, there are actually people and place names that still bear the name in areas the Bari are alleged to have passed through in their sojourns over the centuries. For example, there are communities in both Eritrea and Ethiopia that still bear the name Bari. In any case, whatever they used to call themselves, foreigners who came to Bari country in the early part of the eighteenth century found the Bari referring to themselves as Bari.

Although the two legends agree that the Bari are immigrants, they differ, however, in two crucial respects—the composition of the Bari tribe and the names of the Lakes associated with the final migration into the Nile Valley. While Haddon believes that the Bari are a splinter group of a larger Bari-Berri group, Spagnolo believes them to be a member of a larger Bari-Lotuho-Lokoya tribe. That indeed seems to be the case. Spagnolo cites the following oral tradition, attributed to the Lokoya:

> "Long ago, there was a man called Wotoko. He was lame. He had four wives namely: Igoŋ, Poni, Pita and Sala. Each of the four wives had children. The children of Igoŋ were: Iparaŋ and Okare or Pitya. Poni had: Tombe and Jada; Pita and Sala each had one child.

> One day, when Wotoko was very old and knew that his last days were near, he summoned all his elder sons from his five wives to see him very early one morning so that he may share with them his last wishes. Very early the following morning, one of the sons, Tombe, the son of Poni arrived to see his father, saying, "Father, I have come". "Alright", the old man replied. I give you all my cows. Sometime later in the morning, the second to report to the summons of his father was Iparaŋ, the elder son of Igoŋ. "Iparaŋ, you have come" His father asked. "Yes, father", Ipara replied. "Why did you delay my son? Your brother Tombe was here and I have given him all the cows.
>
> To you, I have nothing, but I leave you with ochre. You will use it to trade for goats with your brother. As for cattle, I have none for you" the old man ended. After Iparaŋ, the son of Pita arrived. His father told him that he had nothing for him since he arrived late.
>
> All he had, he had already distributed it between those of his brothers who reported early. However, he said, "Here is a spoon. Plug it to your head as a horn. It will protect you against those who will hunt you". The last to arrive was the son of Sala. "I have nothing to give you my son. Eat the shrubs and trees. Be a beggar. If they refuse to help, I give you this one hand so that you may beat those who may refuse to give you food or attempt to kill you". Soon after that the old man died. Tombe became the ancestor of the Bari, Lado gave birth to the Lotuho; Iparaŋ became the ancestor of the Lokoya. Thus, the Bari, the Lotuho and Lokoya are brothers according to this legend.

Simonse (1992:51) says that the story offers an explanation for the difference in cattle wealth of the Bari and the Lotuho and of the contrasting life-styles of the Bari and Lakoya respectively. The Bari live in the plains and own cattle, while the Lokoya are goat owners, raiders and live up the mountains.

A similar Lotuho legend—the curse of King Imuhunyi of the Lotuho by his father Attulung, the King of Calamini - also supports a genetic relationship between the Bari and the Lotuho:

"Imuhunyi (*mukunyet*), 'ant' the son of Attulang, the King of Calamini, younger the brother of Subek the King of Ulubari who lived at Li'bu, was cursed by his father. He had many wives but he was not blessed with children. He went to his brother Subek at Li'bu to deliver him from the curse. When he arrived at the palace of the Bari King, the King subjected him to many tests to prove if he was a powerful King.

Satisfied, the King of the Bari now requested him to perform a final feat—to cross the river Nile while smoking his pipe. It would take him four days to do so. Imuhunyi was frightened.

However, his host assured him it would be all right. Reluctantly, he obeyed and walked gingerly into river. He stayed under water for four days. Meanwhile, his assistant was so overcome with grief at what he thought was the loss of his King that he set about wailing, singing a dirge, lamenting the demise of his beloved King.[32] When Imuhunyi emerged, he found Subek waiting for him. He gave him a *lori* or '*Asalak*' (a long pointed spear) and a bull. King Subek instructed Imuhunyi to slaughter the bull for food each time they came to rest, but not to eat the head. He told Imuhunyi to eat the head when the bull stopped walking and there would be where he would establish his own village.

King Imuhunyi did as he was told by his host, King Subek. He called the place where the bull stopped *walking Imatare*."[33]

Both of these stories do not support the theory of Bari-Berri split. Contrary to the Bari-Berri legend, Spagnolo (1933) version posits a different secondary split—a Bari-Lotuho-Lokoya split. According to this, legend, the Bari, Lotuho and the Lokoya originally belonged to one tribe. Surprisingly, however, Espagnolo's own observations contradict this legend. The Spagnolo (1933:275) version of the Bari split suggests that other members of the group that constitutes the Bari, the so called 'Bari-speakers', were, in fact, not genetically related to the Bari at all, especially the Pajulu, Kuku and Nyangwara. These people, he alleges, were originally a part of the Oxoriok (a group of Lokoya related communities). According to him, the Oxoriok was once a large tribe composed of many Lokoya sub-tribes made up of: *Ifwotu, Itang, Imotong, Imoruk, Kuku, Lyangari, Lopit, Nyangwara, Ɖayoro, Ɖulere, O'Bele, O'Frika, O-*

Irya, O-Kire, O-Kömuturu, O-Milin, O-Woi, OXilyo, O-Xityari, O-Xoyni and other less important ones.

Figure 2: *An illustration of Bari activities*

Spagnolo based his arguments on the premise that these groups were physically and culturally different from the Bari proper. Incidentally, this was an observation made by the earlier explorers and other foreigners who visited Bari country at the beginning of the 19th century. The Bari were tall and were pastoralists while the Bari-speaking groups were generally short and were agriculturalists.

As you have seen, there is no direct Bari-Berri connection attested in the reconstruction. The confusion might have arisen in the way the Bari used the term Böri (Berri). The Bari used to call the Berri, *Böri-lo-koro* and the Acholi also *Böri*. In recording the legend, whoever told Haddon the legend did not clarify the dual usage of the word and thus the confusion. In terms of linguistic classification, the *Berri,* or more properly the *Pari* as they now call themselves, are classified as belonging to the Luo group of languages and are grouped together with the Shilluk, Acholi, and Anuak and belong to the western branch of the Nilotic. If there is any *Bari-Börri/Berri* connection, it could only be through their common origin from proto-Nilotic.

Beaton (1934:170–172) holds a similar view. According to Beaton, oral traditions of the Bari indicate that during the reign of one Lokoro, the Rain Chief of Sindiru from about (1605–1625), events occurred to confirm that the 'Bari-speakers' were not a part of the Bari proper.

It all started with the attack on the Bari of Sindiru by the Oxoriok, who according to Spagnolo (1933:XII), consisted of Lokoya sub-tribes made of: Ifwotu, Itang, Imotong, Imoruk, Kuku, Ilyangari, Lopit, Nyangwara, Dayoro, Dulere, O'Bele, O'Frika, O-Irya, O-Kire, O-Kömuturu, O-Milin, O-Woi, OXilyo, O-Xityari, O-Xoyni and other less important ones.[34] Hitherto, the Oxoriok, especially the *Fajulu* and the *Lulubo* had lived at Sindiru in apparent enmity with the Bari. They had, however, secretly coveted the Bari for being in possession of the hills of Sindiru and in such a stronghold of rain power. The Bari used to call the *Fajulu* and the *Lulubo lo mu kudit,* meaning 'those who are as many as grass'. Aware of the rising friction with their neighbours and in a fight that might ensue they may fare badly due to lack of men, the Bari consulted a famous diviner *('bunit*) who lived at *Loike* near Sindiru. The advice of the diviner was that they go by night and tie feathers of white cattle egrets *'kokan'*, to tall treetops both round their dwellings and on hills slopes. 'Next morning, the *Fajulu* and the *Lulubo* awoke with hostile intent, but, when they saw the feathers, they mistook them for the headdress of Bari warriors and, fearing that their plans had been betrayed and that they were surrounded by the enemy—a consternation of which the Bari were not slow to avail themselves - they incontinently fled before a vastly inferior force.'[35] The *Fajulu* directed their flight to the west across the Nile from Sindiru, to where they reside at the present; the *Lulubo* to the east, up the *Lulubo* hills where they now live.[36]

If Beaton and Spagnolo's claim that the 'Bari-Speakers' were not, in fact, Bari is true, then it raises very interesting linguistic, historical and socio-cultural questions. Beaton (1934) and Spagnolo (1933) alleged that they were a collection of sub-tribes of either the Berri (Luo) or the Lokoya also known as the Oxoriok.

Linguistically, cognate counting which is a sure way of determining genetic relatedness between languages shows that the languages these people speak are nothing but variants or dialects of Bari. Furthermore, structural, phonological, semantic and analyses of the groups in the Bari cluster points to nothing other than the fact these clusters are what linguists would call dialects—variations of the same language. If any of these groups were indeed speakers of Lokoya, or any other languages or languages, there would be relics of linguistic evidence left in the language, either in the lexicon or in the phonetics of the language as tell-tales of massive linguistic borrowing from Bari, leading to total linguistic and cultural assimilation of these groups by the Bari. So far, this does not seem to have happened.

For them to have shifted from Oxoriok speakers to exclusive Bari-speakers, two or three things would need to have happened. First, they would have to have been bilingual speakers of both Oxoriok and Bari. Second, this bilingual stage would have to have existed for a long time, resulting in gradual language-shift of many Oxoriok speakers becoming competent and more proficient in Bari rather than in Oxoriok. Overtime, all Oxoriok speakers within the area occupied by the Bari would cease to speak the language and speak Bari only as mother tongue. At this stage, the Oxoriok language would have died and all Oxoriok speakers would have become monolingual Bari speakers within Bari speech area.

If the Bari speakers were indeed originally Lokoya, then the presence of the Lokoya across the border of the Bari and the continued contact between the two groups, though often not in the best of terms, would have acted as a break against these processes: total cultural and linguistic assimilation and language death. Rather, what would have happened would be some sort of syncretism between Bari and Oxoriok cultures and languages. Oddly enough, the Oxoriok language in the guise of Lokoya language is still alive and well and exists in close proximity with Bari. Despite the existence of the conditions that would prevent cultural change and total language shift, it is odd that these Oxoriok speakers would assimilate to become Bari-speakers, if indeed, they did. Could it be possible both Spagnolo and indeed Beaton are mistaken?

While it may well be the case that what were called the Oxoriok constituted a constituent part of the larger proto-eastern Nilotic language family, the genetic comparative method shows definitively that the primary split of proto-eastern Nilotic was into Bari and non-Bari groups. Now the Bari group has remained the six groups since the split, namely; *Bari, Fajulu, Kakwa, Mundari, Kuku and Nyangwara.* One who is familiar with the groups may indeed, well ask, why are there marked physical characteristics between the Bari and the so-called 'Bari-speakers' (*Fajulu, Kakwa, Mundari, Kuku* and *Nyangwara*) and that would be a very fair question. It is not a very easy question to answer, but one may conjecture that the following would seem to have happened.

According to Herodotus (book two:129), the areas of the Nile south of the sudd and the Equatorial forest region were originally inhabited by a race of small and pygmy-type peoples before the desiccation of the Sahara around 7000 BC. The presence of these people along the Nile predated that of the Madi-speaking groups who were later themselves displaced by the arrival of proto-Eastern Nilotics. Thus, the Bari came into the Nile Basin to a place already occupied by these peoples, who they dislodged into areas away from the Nile Valley. As they expanded away to the west, south and south-west of the Nile area, they came into inevitable physical and cultural contacts with the retreating groups. This intermixing of blood, culture and languages resulted in a convergence of these features. One might surmise that it is this convergence of cultural, physical and linguistic traits that led to the emergence of the myth of the so called "Bari-speaking peoples".

As for physical characteristics, these may easily be attributed to intermarriages, either consensual or forced, between the newcomers and the indigenous populations. The newcomers to the area were tall and well built while the natives were small and short. Now it is a scientific fact, in the expression of particular genetic traits in subsequent generations, some genes may be recessive, while other genes may be dominant. Genes that express tallness characteristics may be dominant in the one case while the converse may be true in another instance. The result is that you get a new population type, which is different from the two original donor populations. Thus, although one can find tall people amongst them, generally, the Bari speakers in general are not as tall as the Bari and not as short as the original pygmy or small people type of Herodotus. That is the 'different physical characteristics' between the 'Bari proper' and the 'Bari-speakers' observed by Spagnolo.

One would conjecture that the observed differences in height between the Bari and the "Bari-speaking" tribes are largely attributable to this biological process. This can very easily be shown to be the case. All one needs to do is to visit the Bari-Bari speakers divide. As one moves away from the epicentre of Bari stronghold (central Bari), in an easterly, southerly and westerly directions, there is a noticeable change in general heights of the people in these areas. The people become comparatively shorter on average. However, as one goes north of the Bari stronghold, to areas where there had been little contact with the pygmy type, there is no commensurate reduction in height although intermarriages have also taken place between the Bari and the groups north of them. To the north of the Bari are the Mundari/Sir/Sera and the Dinka. These are of Nilotic origins and are of the same physical type as the Bari.

The Bari of northern Bari and the Mundari of Tali and Gemeza are a very good example. On average the Bari of northern Bari, the area south of Rejaf to Mongolla, are taller than the Bari of southern Bari. The Bari of southern Bari (considered to be the area south of Rejaf) are at the front line with a number of Sudanic groups such as the Madi, Lulubo, Lugbara, Moru and so on with who they have intensely intermarried. The Mundari of Tali border the Dinka to the north and the Moru to the south. Generally, those Mundari who got married to Moru to the south, tend on average to be shorter than the Mundari who married into Dinka families to the north. The Dinka and the Mundari belong to the same racial type. They tend to have the same physical characteristics. The same is true of the Bari who married a Mundari in Gemeza to the north, and vice versa.

Cultural difference

The 'proper Bari' and the 'Bari-speakers' are culturally different because, according to the proponents of this theory the 'Bari proper' have cattle, while the 'Bari-speaking' tribes have none. If that is all there is to this argument, then the argument is false. If the possession of and non-possession of cattle amounts to a major cultural difference then, one can also rightly claim that the Bari of southern Bari are culturally different from those of northern Bari because the former have cattle while the latter do not. Of course, anyone who knows the composition of this group would know this conclusion to be patently false.

What seemed to have happened was that the Bari, who moved into the areas occupied by the retreating peoples, lost their cattle and other animals to cattle theft by the Turco-Egyptians in 1821, the slave traders and to tsetse-fly infestation. This is true of the people of southern Bari as well as the other so-called Bari speakers. To this day, in fact, like the so-called 'proper Bari' most of their songs are about cattle and their 'bride-price' is still conducted in terms of cattle, although they do not have cattle anymore.

Another possible reason why the Bari on the cultural contact areas (the Bari-speakers) lost their cattle, leading to cultural change, could be due to disinterest in cattle keeping or loss of knowledge of cattle keeping. Many of the conquered indigenous people in the area did not possess cattle anyway. These people were either hunter-gatherers or agriculturists. That being the case, it would be absurd for one to expect them to be interested in cattle. It is likely that the newcomers might have been influenced by their hosts and adapted to their hosts' ways of live.

In this view, contrary to Spagnolo's position, the so called Bari speakers are actually Bari, albeit mixed Bari. In that connection, contrary to what may be believed, the Fajulu, Kakwa, Mundari, Nyangwara and Kuku are, in fact, an offshoot of the main Bari group, rather than a subjugated or an assimilated group. As matter of fact, according to oral traditions, these groups were part of Bari war formation units deployed to the front during the occupation of the Nile Basin. The *'kikwa'* (thorns) which became corrupted to

Kakwa were, in fact, a name given to the unit sent to secure the southwest region. The *"oŋgwora"* (horns), 'Nyangwara' was the force that was dispatched to fight on the western front. The Kuku were known as *"kùkù"* (to pierce). There is nothing unusual in the fact that one of the component group or groups might have at one time or other allied with other hostile group or groups against one of its own.

This is a historical as well as a political fact. Societies do that all the time. In view of the fact that the Fajulu and Nyangwara at one time (1605–1625) sided with the Oxoriok against the Bari should not be construed to mean that they were not a part of that tribe. These kinds of alliance are the norm rather than the exception in volatile political situations. Oral traditions collected in Liria suggest that the Bari-speaking groups were staying near Liria, to the east of Sindiru. They started to migrate westwards towards Nyangwaraland west of the Nile in the beginning of the nineteenth century (Simeone 1992:163).

The gradual drying up of the plains between the Didinga Hills and Lake Turkana triggered mass migration and interethnic wars. According to Webster (1977), this is considered a starting point in many migrations myths, not only to the east but also to the south. Mount Lotuke, the eastern tip of the Didinga Hills is the place with permanent water. Here communities fought each other for the control of this resource: the Lotuho-speaking peoples and the *Pari* opposed the *Toposa, Didinga* and *Narim*; to the west of the Lotuho, the Lotuho came face to face against the *Ohoriok (Oxoriok)* who were in turn opposed by the Bari.

With pressure mounting from the east, for land and water, particularly from the Ohoriok, the Bari-speaking groups moved west of the Nile. In this general militarized situation, the Bari in turn formed a military threat to their eastern neighbours. They are alleged to have initiated war against the Kuku and Nyepo, while the Kuku, Kakwa and Fajulu in their turn expanded into the territory occupied by the speakers of Madi-Moru Languages.

6

The Bari Before the Invasion (1500–1840)

In this chapter, we consider the early history of the Bari people dating from time immemorial to their first contact with the foreigners—Turco-Egyptian invasion in 1841. This period will cover the emergence and the rise of Rain Chiefs (*Kimak ti Piong*) and the decline of traditional chiefs (*Kimak ti kak*) and the attendant conflicts that arose from competition for rainmaking power by the new pretenders to the throne.

Early settlement

It is not easy to date precisely the coming of the Bari into the Nile Basin. This will have to wait for the development of more precise techniques such as carbon dating of archaeological digs. We will for the time being however, rely on oral history, which is also a relatively reliable tool for determining historical events and dates.

Proto-Nilotes existed around the third millennium B.C. At about one B.C. this group had separated into proto-western Nilotic, proto-Eastern Nilotic and proto-Southern Nilotic. This separation took over 1000 years. If the time depth that marks the separation between two nodal communities is approximated to be 1000 years, then one can assume that it must have taken the same time for the Bari group to separate from the non-Bari group from proto-Eastern Nilotic. Thus if proto-Eastern Nilotic was born at about one millennium B.C., proto-Bari must have been born by about 1000 A.D. Bari remembered history begins to emerge at about 1500 A.D. Let us suppose that the early centuries between 1000 and 1500 A.D. were given to migration, settlement, expansion and consolidation.

The territory occupied by the Bari-speaking people extends over an area approaching a rectangle some 160 miles in length, extending southwards from latitude 6° 5´, and having a maximum breadth of some 90 miles. The territory lies to the south of the Dinka country embracing both banks of the river. To the east of this area are to be found the Lotuho, Lokoya and the Lulubo; to the extreme south, the Madi; to the west, the Muru, Lugbra and other Sudanic peoples.

Early remembered history of the Bari shows that the centres of power in Bariland were at Sindiru in the far south of Bariland and Ilibari and Bilinyang to the north. It is uncertain when the Bari first settled in the area, but one can conjecture that that should be around the 1100 or 1200 AD, or thereabouts because by about the beginning of early fifteenth and mid-sixteenth century, remembered oral tradition of the Bari people began to emerge. From this remembered history and tradition, it is possible to reconstruct the history of the Bari by tracing particularly the history of the Bari of Sindiru, Gondokoro and Bilinyang. These three centres are crucial to the understanding of the history of Bari people before the coming of the foreigners to Bari land. Furthermore, these centres are important because they are closely associated with the history of rain making dynasties, especially of one of the largest Bari Rain Making clans, the 'Bekat Limat' clan. Compared to the other Bari clans, the *Bakat* clan has been unique in that it has meticulously kept the activities of its ancestors, particularly those of its rainmaking chiefs, through oral tradition. This oral history has been invaluable in the reconstruction of the early history of the Bari people before the coming of foreigners to Bariland.

We are particularly fortunate in that connection because the early Europeans, have already done a lot of work— collecting oral history of the Bari people, particularly writers like Beaton (1934), Whitehead (1921), Haddon (1911), Mouteney-Jephson (1890), Spagnolo (1933) and others. Of all researchers who have worked on Bari history, Beaton (1934) and Spagnolo (1933) stand out. They have compiled an enormous amount of data on the oral history and traditions of the Bari as related by serving members of the tribe.

The history of rainmaking dynasty is central to Bari history because it provides easily datable genealogical information. Beaton (1934) and Spagnolo (1933) are invaluable sources because they particularly recognized the need to record oral traditions as remembered by its surviving members. The Rain Making clans, especially the Bekat clan at Sindiru, was famous among the Bari for being the only family among the Bari which can trace its ancestry far back, and which has preserved traditions even of it most distant ancestors.

It is not until the arrival of the Bakat Limat that there emerges a myth relating to the movements of the Bari prior to their arrival from the Nile Valley. As will become evident, traditions of this clan reach way back over fourteen generations, roughly about 250 years. What the Bari lacked, the Europeans provided—the dating of these genealogies.

The early chronology of the Bekat is an educated guess, but to arrive at a probable date, Beaton used the arrival of the first European in Bariland as a starting point for recorded Bari history. He proceeded as follow: Mr. Thibault (1840) saw and talked to Loguno lo Muludyang, who was then the King of Bilinyang and Ilibari in 1840. Loguno died in 1860. Another European explorer, Morlang, saw Nyiggilo, who was then king after the death of his father. He reasoned that if Nyiggilo became king 15 years before 1840, Muludyang might have died about 1825. Allowing 20 years to a generation, it becomes a straightforward matter to determine the duration of each subsequent reign from, for example, Dere (1805), Sube (1785) and so on. This was also the methodology used to determine the periodization of the history of Ilibari/Bilinyang.[37]

On the Sindiru line, however, determining historical dates was based on the activity of 'government' chiefs while in office. Working backwards and calibrating the stories remembered by living members of the clan, it was possible to work out the history of the Bekat Limat. Based on this regressive calculation, we can estimate the beginning of remembered Bari history to be between 1200 A.D. and 1500 A.D.

Remembered history of Bari people begins with Sindiru, which the Bari consider to be their cradle. Sindiru is the name of a hill on the East of the White Nile about 40 miles south of Juba. It is the traditional home of the Bekat Limat line of Rain Chiefs 'whose repute was great, not only among the Bari, but also among the

Fujulu and north among the Mundari. It is also reputed to be the cradle of the Bari Tribe' (Beaton 1934:169).

The beginning of remembered history of the Bari begins with the Bekat clan who, due to their claim to possession of rain making powers and the importance attached to ran-making, had reason to revere their past rain chiefs. The Bekat claim that their original homeland was around the present Sindiru Hills and their earliest ancestor was a rainmaker called '*Yo 'yok*'.

'Yo'yok (about 1565–1585)

Based on the criteria for dating events, '*Yo 'yok* would have lived from about 1565–1585. He was alleged to have gotten his powers for rainmaking miraculously from the God of Heaven *(Ngun lo-ki)* who declared him the lord of all rainmakers. This would place the period the Bekat clan settled at Sindiru at about (1565–1585). However, this presupposes that the clan came into the area with this social structure intact. Suppose that this rain making culture was a new a phenomenon, a trait acquired after years of wondering in drought - stricken areas and, therefore, the need to have supernatural control over rain production. If true, the culture would have to be rooted in the culture of the people in time. This would take time, at least, three to four generations, that is about 80 years, if a generation is twenty years, or 140 years if a generation is about 35 years.

Depending on the estimate, it would require at least 80 or 140 years to instill the new culture of rainmaking into the general culture of the community. This would place the time of settlement somewhere around the early twelfth (1165 A.D.) or late fifteenth century, around 1485 A.D.[38] In fact, traditions collected by Buxton (1963) and others from the Pari, a people of Luo descent, would seem to imply rainmaking was foreign to the Bari. A Luo speaking people who had lived in the place the Bari now occupy brought the skill. According to one of the traditions collected by Buxton, rainmaking was foreign to the Bari. It came to them through the Nyori Clan which was alleged to have been of Luo origin. Buxton cites two traditions he collected from the Böri in support of his claim.

According to this tradition, the *Böri/Berri* and the *Anuak* were once one people. However, the *Böri/Berri* split from the *Annuak* at *Wi-Pari,* a place near *Kit River,* which flows through the southern part of Bariland into the Nile, not far from Sindiru. According to the tradition, from *Kit,* the village through which the river flowed, the Annuak went east, while the *Böri/Berri* went west of the Nile to present day *Terekeka* in Mundari land.

The second tradition again collected by Buxton (1963:5) at Körisomba, in the Terekeka area, reports of successive separation of four brothers who originally lived at Liria. These brothers belonged to a rainmaking clan. When the brother who controlled rain withheld it from the others, the three moved away and became the founding ancestors of the Böri living alongside the Nile, Köbura, a section of the Mundari, and the Pari of Lafon. The Pari were expelled later from Liria by the Ohoya (Lakoya).

The expulsion of the Pari from Liria

'Before the arrival of Hatulang, the leader of the Ohoyo (Lotuho-speaking invaders from the East) the Pari and Omoholony (the later Ongole) lived on Opone hill. The Onyoke—who according to some informants spoke Bari— lived on the hills across the pass. The Pari and Onyoke had interminable fights over the use of the water of the Hicoroi stream. The Pari had sharpened sticks, the Onyoke fought with iron weapons. Hatulang united the Onyoke and the clans that followed him and ordered fires to be lit in a large semi-circle at the foot of the mountain so that the Pari believed they were outnumbered. Many of the Pari who tried to break through the cordon were killed, the others fled to Lafon. Only a few blind people were left behind in Liria where their descendants live up to the present day" (Buxton 1963, quoted from Simeone (1992: 55)).

Considered together with Haddon's story about an alleged Barri-Bari split and the migration of Chief Tombe of the Nyori clan to Nile Basin, one can deduce that the Nyori clan rainmaking tradition probably predates that of the Bekat Clan. If that is true, then 'Yo'yok could not have been the first rainmaker of the Bari.

Unfortunately, unlike the Baket, the Nyori did not keep a meticulous record of their rainmaking ancestors. Because the Bekat have kept a faithful record of their ancestors, that record has been extremely useful in the reconstruction of the history of the rest of the Bari tribe as a whole.

Lomijikotet (about 1585–1605)

'Yo'yok was succeeded by his son Lomijikotet. While 'Yo 'yok got his rainmaking prowess from the god of heaven, Lomijikotet was born with a rain-stone tightly clenched in each hand. He was thus born a Rain King.

There seems to be some confusion in the name and genealogy of Lomijikotet. In addition to the Bekat, these two are also claimed to be the progenitors of two other clans, namely: *Dung Kaliri* and *Nyori Kimak*. Spagnolo (1933:278) gives a different name to *Lomijikotet* (literally, the one with the tail of the rat) as *'Dirmiji'*—and he interprets it as meaning 'one who knows each and everything'—"*adi 'dinya lo'dirja kulya adi mit*". Beaton (1934:170) points out that Spagnolo seems to have confused the early genealogy of the Sindiru line. He observes that although Spagnolo lists the names *lomijikotet,* '*Kuwuba*' (as famous as his father) and '*Pintong*' as belonging to the Sindiru line, rather, they belonged to two other lines of Rain Chiefs—*Kogi* and *Pager.*

At Kogi, to the south of Sindiru, was a secondary Rain-making clan called the Dungkaliri, which also numbers the Chief among its ranks. This section claimed Lomijikotet to be their ancestor. In addition, at a place called Pipiri, one of the villages of Pager, a section of Nyori Kimak clan also claims progeny to Lomijikotet. In this line, Lomijikotet appears thirteen generations earlier, where Kuwuba, Pintong and Lokuryeje also occur, but not in the same position as at Sindiru.

Beaton argues that there is no legend that points to Lomijikotet as being the founder of all three families of Rain Chiefs. It is equally impossible to suppose that the *Bekat, Dung* and *Nyori* clans divided off from one original clan. If that were the case, the name of the original clan would normally be preserved in the sub-clan as a distinguisher; thus *Bekat Kimak* are a section of the *Bekat, Nyori Kimak*, a section of the *Nyori* clan and *Dung Kaliri*, a section of the *Dung* clan. There is no common origin to the *Bekat, Dung* and *Nyori* clans. Beaton (1934) concludes that perhaps, there is a mythical line of ancestors or at any rate, one legendary ancestor of Rain Chiefs, to whom they refer their origin in much the same way as the ancient Greeks used to trace their descent from their own legendary heroes.

Lokoro (about 1605–1625)

Lokoro became Rain Chief after his father Lomijikotet, but his reign was marred by serious social upheaval that would eventually split the Bari at Sindiru and set in motion a set of events that would nearly destroy the Bari as a people.

Kuwuba (about 1625–1645)

Lokoro was succeeded by his son Kuwuba about 1625–1645. However, nothing much seemed to have happened during his reign until the rule of his son Pintong who was Rain Chief after him.

Pintong (about 1645–1665)

Pintong was chief from about 1645–1665 and his fame spread far and wide. He was reputed to be a just and wise Rain King. Even up to today, the Bari still use him for dating events and reverently refer to him with the saying that '*ge ge ko Pintong*', meaning since the time of Pintong. The following story is told to illustrate his sagacity:

Pitnong and Lokuryeje

> "There was once long ago, a man called Pintong, who originally came from the North.[39] One day, as he was sitting down, he brooded in his heart, saying, 'There are many diviners in the land, but how may I discover those that are good?' Then he chose a small house and put his firestones inside it, and took a small pot, poured water in it with some beans, stood it on the stones and lit a fire with ebony wood.

Then he cried out with a loud voice, and selecting two servants, he sent them to call a diviner. When the diviner came, he said, "Your ancestor is angry with you. Choose a bull quickly and slay it', and Pintong said: 'Good, take this goat and go home'. After that he sent a messenger to fetch another diviner, who came and said: 'Cook a sacrifice to your grandmother.' After that he sent for another diviner but he, too was baffled and all the others who were summoned were baffled. Then he sent his servants to call a man of great renown, whose name was Tombe Lokuryeje. Now Tombe has two houses afar off, and the one belonged to this wife and the other to that. When the messengers approached the more distant house they asked the woman, saying: 'Where is your husband?' But she merely motioned with her head signifying 'Over there'. At this moment he heard them and came hurrying up. His path was in the air and he walked on a spider's web. When he came up he said: 'Where are you going? I knew my wife had nodded here. Go on! I know all your words. You came with seven hoes, and hid one of them, leaving six'. They said: 'But these six are the only ones'. He replied: 'Not so. Go on, please'. And when they reached home, Lukuryeje said: 'Go over there,' and when they had obeyed, he said: 'Strike beneath this shrub! What is this? Is this not the hoe you hid?'

Then those messengers dug out the hoe and went home. Then Lokuryeje took a goat and said: 'Here, go your ways, and cook this on the road, but be sure not to cook the head; put that in a basket. Then when you draw near to your homes, cook everything with the head. I shall remain with you four days, and then on the fifth I shall arrive. And when you hear the earth shaking as with an earthquake, perhaps that will be me arriving'. They departed and when they came to the place where they intended to sleep, they killed the goat, and put the head in the basket. The head turned into a goat. Next day they moved on, and in the evening, when they were near home, they cut the goat's throat and ate its head and all. When they reached Pintong's house, they told him all that they had seen, and at that moment Lokuryeje arrived and said; 'Why do you keep your beans on the fire until they smell? Bring flour to that house, and cook it that we may eat'.

He then went to sleep. Next morning he arose and called Pintong out on to flat rock, and the knees and legs of Lokuryeje sank therein. Then he gave orders, saying: 'My fishermen are coming, they follow the river. They are white, but do not be afraid. At that time you shall beget Chiefs large of head, of whom you shall call one Wani Yemba 'Dija'.[40] And in the future your daughters shall bear their first child while still young'. And Pintong said: 'If our daughters bear their children while still young, how will their descendants fare?' Lokuryeje replied: 'Their descendants will bear first child when no bigger than flies.' Pintong asked: 'But if they bear children when no bigger than flies, what of their posterity?' Lokuryeje replied: 'Then shall the race be brought to an end' (Spagnolo 1933:276–277).

Lokuryeje's orders to Pintong were as ironical as they were prophetic. While he correctly prophesied the coming of the white man to Bari country and the route through which he would come, he did not warn Pintong of the danger that this would pose to his people. Lokuryeje's admonitions to Pintong to 'not to be afraid' were ironic because, in fact, he should have warned him to be afraid. As we shall see in subsequent chapters, all the apprehensions Pintong expressed in his nervous questioning of Lokuryeje, in fact became true nearly three centuries later. The destruction of the Bari people by the coming of 'the peaceful white children of Lokureje' would make Col. Martyr (1899), a colonial administrator in Uganda, to declare and to propose to his superiors that the Lotuho and the Lokoya resettle the Bari country because, as he points out:[41]

"The warlike and troublesome Bari with whom Baker had so much trouble, are extinct, having been either murdered or taken off as slaves by the Dervishes (sic Ansar). Formerly the country must have been thickly populated for the remains of old villages are very numerous".

In Pitnong's days too, a large number of men whom they called lomukudit, meaning those who are as many as grass, invaded the Bari. Spagnolo (1933:278) tells of a story how Lokuryeje was again called upon by Pintong to save the people.

"They advanced to the west and sacked all the villages on their route. They burnt the hill village of *Ngangala,* called *Lili.*

> They defeated the Bari who scattered abroad in distant villages, both to the east and the west of the Nile and to the south. Pintong fetched for Lokuryeje saying: 'Come, drive away the Lomukudit'. And Lokuryeji replied: 'Take those two sons of yours called Mödi; take one Mödi to Pitya (which is a mountain towards Lowe) and let him go and thrust his Iron Bar (*Lori*) into the earth there; and let the other Mödi go west of the Nile together with a man from the *Mingi* clan.' Thus were these two men called Mödi divided, and they broke off reeds from the swamps to use as spears. The one dashed forward shaking his spear and the other did likewise, so that the force of Lomukudit was completely broken and disappeared to the west, and the land was saved.
>
> Then the villages which have scattered and hid in the grass assembled together again under the leadership of Pintong."

According to Beaton, Spagnolo conjectures this to have been the Galla incursion in the seventeenth century. If true then the dates here ascribed to Pintong are perhaps correct. If so, the mass dispersal that took place between 1885 and 1898 where the Bari were scattered to the east, west, and south of their areas, in addition to being divided into three countries was probably different. This would be the second time the Bari have been dispersed from their homes.

Tombe Lokureje (about 1665–1685): The golden age in Bariland

Lokuryeje assumed the mantle of chieftainship from his father, Pintong.[42] Tombe Lokureje's reign was the golden age in Bari history. Never has there been such prosperity in the land. During Lokureje's rule, there was unparalleled peace and prosperity in Bariland. With their enemies vanquished and on the run, the Fajulu chased to a safe distance across the Nile from Sindiru, the Lulubö up the hills and the Lomukudit dispelled from Bari land, Lokureje's reign was considered the golden age in Bari history. There was universal peace and prosperity all across the length and breadth of Bari land. There was plenty of rain. The land was rich and fertile. The women were blessed with fertility, too. The fecundity of their herd was such that it has never been surpassed since. The land was very heavily populated. The lives of the people were organized around cattle:

> "During the wet season the Bari cattle were driven inland to places where the grass was good. At one time, the Bari villages on the west bank of the Nile between Rejaf and the River Luri used to take their herds all the way to the River Ko'da. There a kurumi (a large cattle enclosure) was built of posts of ebony wood (pöyöt) thorns. The 'teton' (young men) of eighteen to thirty five years of age remained with the cattle while the married men, women and children stayed at home, and the young girls journeyed backwards and forwards carrying milk. The warriors herded cattle by day and danced and sang songs by night. Their food during the time was for the most part milk, blood drawn from the necks of the cow and mixed with milk and a little dura."[43]

This scenario was repeated throughout Bari land. Lokureje was revered. He was hardly ever seen outside his house unless on special occasions. Only on very rare occasions would he grant audience to distinguished elders but only after the payment of a ram, or a bull as a suppliant offering. The privileged elder had to come 'with eyes abased and crawling abjectly on the ground.'

As is the natural order of things, Tombe Lokuryeje died around 1685. His death heralded the death, of the golden age in Sindiru and in Bari.

Mödi Lokuryeje (about 1685–1705)

When Lokureje died, the mantle of Lokureje fell on his son, Mödi Lokureje who tried hard to preserve his father's legacy, but unlike his father, he appeared often in public. During the last days of Lokureje rule, trouble was brewing between rivaling villages, Kogi and Sindiru, which eventually erupted into an open war during the time of Mödi Lokureje.

Sindiru had sought help from its traditional enemy, the Lulubo, in its plot to destroy Kogi. In alliance with the Lulubo, Sindiru attacked *Wado Lomijikotet* who lived at a place called *Wordiang* near Kogi. In the ensuing battle, Wado was heavily routed and was forced to flee into exile to an island in the Nile called Rume, where his son named Rume was born to him.

Tome Mödi (1705–1725)

As the gods would have it, Mödi Lokuryeje died in exile. Fortunately for Kogi, Wado's very able son *Rume,* became chief. From the island, Rume raised an army and marched to *Kogi* putting to flight the occupying army of Sindiru. The re-occupation of Rume's family home at Wordiang at Kogi was left to Mogaki, Wado's son.

Mödi (1725–1745)

Mödi, the son of Tombe married two wives. The first wife bore a son called Jada and the second wife had two children, a son Manabur and a girl Juwan.

In spite of the civil war between Kogi and Sindiru, the Bari continued to prosper during the successive reigns of Tombe (about 1705–1725) and Mödi (1725–1745). During the reign of Tombe, for example, prosperity continued. As a Rain Chief it was his duty to sit in at every '*putet*' (council convened to make decisions on important matters of state) and to offer counsel to the assembled elders. 'Tombe gained a great reputation for the sagacity of his counsel and the justice of his decisions. His name as arbitrator spread far and wide, and he received many bulls as fees for settling disputes. He grew very rich' (Beaton 1934:174).

The split of Sindiru (c.1745–1815)

Another era worthy of note in Sindiru was from 1745–1845. Mödi Lo-Tombe assumed power after the death of his father Tombe. Although there was relative peace and prosperity, dark clouds were again gathering over Sindiru. The continued raids by the Oxoriok resulting in loss of cattle and many men in battle caused socio-political faults that finally led to the split of Sinduri. From between 1745 and 1765, Mödi assumed the chieftainship of Sindiru from Jada, his father.

When Jada assumed rain chieftainship, calamity struck Sindiru. The rains did not fall on the fields for many years. Crops became parched and blighted. The herds diminished rapidly and the women were barren. Now to arrest the march of these disasters was the first duty of the Rain Chief in order to avert general discontent. When all his attempts, including, invocations to his ancestors to avert the disasters failed, chief Jada resorted to extreme measures. To entice back the rain, to give richness to the soil and to break the spell that lay on their women, *Jada Lo Mödi* ordered his half sister, *Juan na-Mödi* to be buried alive.

Now Manabur, Juan's brother, loved his sister so much so that her sacrifice disgusted him to the extent that he found it virtually impossible for him to stay on in the village they had grown up in together. It was much more intolerable because the decision of the Rain Chief was backed up by public opinion, a decision which he was powerless to either oppose or reverse. He was so overcome with anger and downcast with grief that he could no longer tolerate the sight of the village where they had grown up together. He felt the best course of action was to leave the village altogether. Summoning his sons and daughters, and gathering his cattle together, he moved off to Kuli to found a new section of the Bekat. This came to be known as the Bekat Manabur Section of the Bekat clan.

Now, it is the practice that when a clan becomes too large, it usually divides to admit intermarriage between the sections. However, when the division is over some hurt, such as incest or fratricide, intermarriage is disallowed. This seems to have been the case between the Bekat Limat and Baket Manabur. Even today, these two sections of the Bekat do not intermarry.

Split of Sindiru and the Bilinyang rain dynasty (1765–1785): Subek-lo-Jada

Soon after the split at Sindiru and the founding of the Bekat Manabur section by Manabur, a further division took place at Sindiru. This time the split was between the sons of Jada. Jada had died soon after the disagreement with his half brother over the death of Juan. Fortunately for Jada, he was survived by two able sons, Subek and Kose. Subek was the elder and Kose his junior. The two sons were both capable Rain Chiefs, although Kose the junior appeared to be the better of the two. The rains appeared to obey Kose more than they did Subek. Not wanting to lose face and reputation, Subek opted to move out of Sindiru in quest for adventure and greener pastures.

Calling upon some of his relatives and dependents and a substantial number of warriors to join him, and collecting his cattle, Subek set off to the north. In the course of time, his wanderings led him to the large and hilly village of Bilinyang, which was ruled by Lako 'Doggale, from the Panygillo clan. At Bilinyang, Subek's fortunes changed.

Meanwhile Kose was left in charge of affairs at Sindiru. The enemies of the Bari, the Oxoriok, were quick to exploit Subek's departure from Sindiru. Knowing that he had taken with him a substantial number of warriors from Sindiru, the war-like Oxoriok from the Liria and Tologu hills allied themselves with the perennial enemies of the Bari, the Luluba, and attacked Kose at Sindiru, raiding for cattle. So few were the warriors on account of Subek's departure and the demise of many warriors of the previous reign that Kose had to resort to magic to aid his troops:[44]

> "He restrained his forces on the hill crests until the enemy was upon him. They were misled by the lack of resistance and elated by the small numbers of the enemy ranged against them.
>
> Advancing in an undisciplined manner to what they thought an easy victory, their ranks were all the more thrown out, when suddenly a great wind blew against them and a red mist began to shroud their foes and to creep down the hill slopes. Into these disordered troops the small Bari Company charged and routed them with great slaughter".

The route notwithstanding, the Oxoriok and their allies did not cease cattle raids on the Bari. The raids continued well into the reign of Jangara who reigned from about 1785 to 1815.

Sindiru about 1500 (*an illustration*)

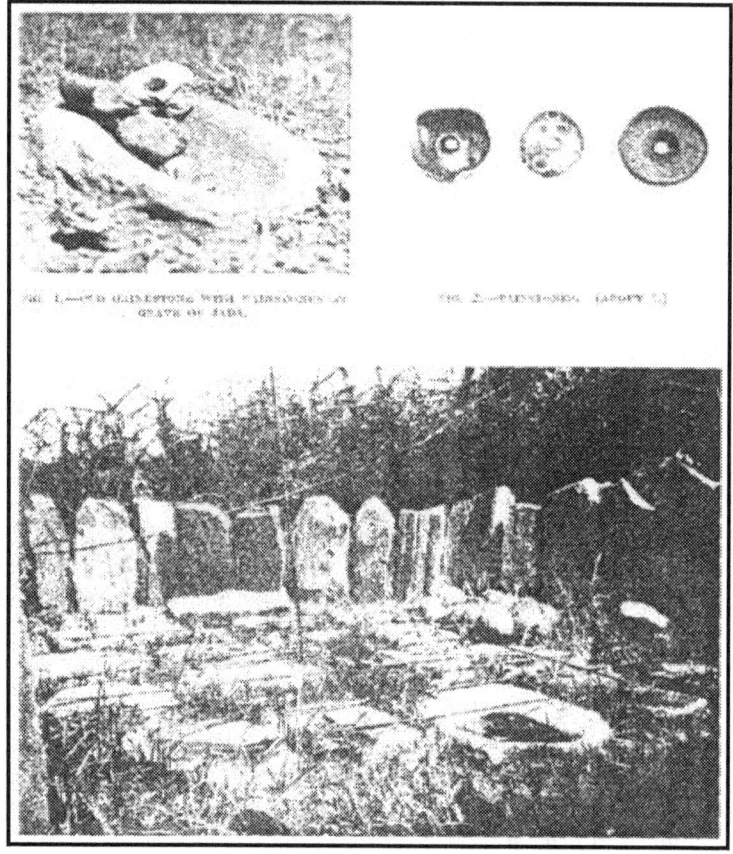

Source: Journal of the Royal Anthropological Institute, Vol. LVIII, 10281 Plate XLVII

Jangara (1785–1815)

Jangara was another renowned Bari Rain Chief. During his time, he had to contend with incessant cattle raids from the Oxoriok. The dearth of manpower continued to be a source of weakness and insecurity for the Bari at Sindiru because it gave their enemies, the Oxoriok, the confidence that they would eventually, drive them out of the coveted rain making centre—Sindiru or deprive them of their life-blood, cattle. In Jangara, however, the Oxoriok met a worthy adversary, a man with prodigious military prowess.

The story is told that in one such raid, Jangara held off his men and let the enemy loot and pillage until they were on their way home. Dividing his forces into two, he fell on the enemy on both flanks recapturing the cattle intact. He was not, however, able to defeat the enemy completely. He was forced to a costly rear-guard action against an Oxoriok rally. The Oxoriok regrouped and harried his men on their way back home. Thus although Jangara recaptured all the raided cattle by the enemy, he left many dead on the battlefield. The loss was so great that the whole of Sindiru was in mourning; the women mourned the loss of their husbands and their beloved sons and reproached Jangara bitterly for causing the death of so many men.

> "The Oxoriok, they cried, "had carried off their cattle; the girls would lament that thus their marriages would be postponed. It was true that Jangara had recovered the cattle but what good were cows, when their owners lay dead on the battle field, and would no more go wooing for marriage" (Beaton 1934:177).

Stun by this criticism, Jangara withdrew to himself and from the war. He sat by as the Oxoriok emptied the cattle kraals of the Bari. Delighted by Jangara's policy of non-resistance, the Oxoriok continued to make a sport of periodically raiding Bari cattle, while the Bari watched helplessly. The raids continued well into the reign of Pitya, the son of Jangara at about 1815, who brought them to an end.

Pitya-lo-Jangara (1815–1845)

Pitya was not a pacifist like his father. He took a belligerent stand towards the raiders. His bellicose stance was bolstered with the fact that public opinion had veered considerably from the attitude that had forced Jangara to adopt a passive policy towards the Oxoriok.

Pitya found that he could rally on Sindiru forces. Although Pitya succeeded in repelling the Oxoriok from Sindiru, he could not, however, defeat them altogether on account of their superior numbers. However, noticing that the enemy was only interested in cattle, he concentrated instead on cultivating grain. He was fortunate in that because during his time, there was so much rain that he was called *Pitia yeng ko piong* 'Pitia who sleeps with water'. Spagnolo (1933:278), translated into English in Beaton (1934:177), attributes a different origin to the name. According to Spagnolo:

> "Lado Jangara (i.e. Jangara Kose) begot two sons who were twins, one called Pitya and the other, Luwala. Pitya was malformed since both his shoulders were short, and his father took him and exposed him in a cave on the mountain, and only had Luwala suckled. After a few days, Luwala died. One day the mother went wandering over the mountain saying: "I will go and look for my son, whether he be alive or dead." She searched and found him sitting in the middle of the water playing there. She thereupon hurled away the stones into the bush, gave him suck and took him back home. When she returned, she talked to Jangara's serf, who was called Swaka, "Lo, the child you took away to the mountain is alive; but if you agree, I have still a little milk in your breast; is it good?" and Swaka replied: "It is good, bring him home," and then he told the father who said: "Verily, it is good. Go bring him home." So the child was brought back and his mother spoke, saying: "Listen, all ye Bari, how did this child survive up on the mountain? How did he endure hunger? He survived by water alone. Let him be suckled. He will become your Rain Chief." Then the child was taken into the house and put to the breast, which he refused. The people cried out, "Bring a bull", and after a sacrificial bull had been led round the child, it accepted the breast. Then the people said: This is he who shall be our Chief." (Spagnolo 1933:278).

In the course of time, Pitya succeeded his father. He sought his wife among his own people and married a Bari girl, called Igale.

Delighted at Jangara's policy of non-resistance, the Oxoriok continued to make periodical raids on the Bari cattle, but in Pitya, they met a very different adversary. Public opinion had veered considerably from the attitude that led to Jangara's passive policy, and Pitia found he could rally the Sindiru forces. He hotly contested the capture of every single bull, without avail. However, as the Oxoriok forces were far superior, during his forlorn sally to guard the kraals, he noticed that the invaders were too intent on carrying off the cattle to trouble themselves with the corn, which they neither burned nor looted. He, therefore, applied himself to the task of invoking the rain, so that hunger at any rate should not stalk through their midst with poverty. The rain fell and the corn stood so thick about the villages that Pitia was affectionately called *Pitia Yeng ko Piong" (Pitia* sleeps with water).

The decline of Sindiru (1845–1885)

Lugör-lo-Pitya

After Pitya, came Lugör. During Lugör's time, there was again a civil war between Kogi and Sindiru. Lugör, recalling the defeat of Kogi and alarmed by the increased population there, went to Köri, the son of Swökiri, at Kogi and suggested that they, as Rain Chiefs, cause a one year's drought in their respective villages to induce famine in order to reduce the number of their burgeoning populations. Secretly, Lugör hoped that this stratagem would harm his rival more than it does him. Köri accepted the proposal but did not honour his part of the deal. Rain continued to fall in Kogi and Kogi cultivated a lot of grain.

Lugör sent a spy to Kogi to find out if Köri was keeping his side of the bargain, but the spy was bribed to report back to Swökiri that it had not rained at Kogi and that there was severe drought and famine. Again, a second spy was sent but he was gain bribed to report the opposite of what was happening on the ground. The grain was safely gathered and stored when a third spy arrived. He was given a basket full of grain with these words: "Take this to Lugör and tell him that our granaries are full."

When Lugör heard that he had been duped, he was incensed and assembling an entourage of eighty men and women, set out to pay Köri a visit at Kogi. Instead of asking for an explanation for his conduct, he demanded for the bride price of *Röuŋ,* a relative of Lugör whom Swökiri, the great-great father of Köri, had married but without completing paying the pride price. To avoid a feud, Köri gave Lugör the eighty cows he wanted. However, not satisfied, Lugör demanded that Köri give him men to go and work his fields as he was short of field hands. Köri closed the discussion by a curt, "I gave you eighty cows."

Lugör returned home slowly, planning how to teach Köri an unforgettable lesson. Reading Lugör's mind, Köri sent word ahead to his people to watch Lugör on his way home and gave them secret orders to meet any attempt by him to take any cattle along the way by force. At a place called *Melukian*, Lugör tried to do just that, but he was promptly attacked and his eighty-men entourage completely wiped out. The eighty women in his retinue were, however, spared. The cattle were confiscated but Lugör and his eighty women were allowed to continue home unharmed, but very humiliated.

Lugör again contrived to return to Kogi, but this time, at the head of an army to punish Köri, for this impertinence. Unfortunately for him, he found Kogi prepared. In the battle that ensued, he was again roundly defeated. Not accepting defeat, Lugör now called on his allies from *Minge*, the chief of the Oxoriok village of *Ilangari* and *Lado*, the son of *Ide,* who, as a descendant of the emigrant Subek, was a relative of Lugör's at Bilinyang.

In response to the threat, Köri also rallied his troops from *Morsak*, *Kogi*, and *Wurkiteng* and further help from *Rombe Agota at Nyarjua*. In the resulting battle, Köri successfully opposed Lugör. Realizing that they were supporting a lost cause, Lugör's allies withdrew from battle, leaving him alone. Taking full advantage of this turn of events on the battlefield, Köri's attack dealt such a blow on the forces of Sindiru that to this day the men of Sindiru are few in number. Kogi did not enjoy his victory over Sindiru for long, however, for this sweet victory over its mortal enemy coincided with the emergence on the scene of an even more implacable and dangerous enemy— the Arab invasion.

Finding both Sindiru and Kogi weakened by internal strife and internecine intertribal wars, and having lost so many able-bodied men in these senseless battles, both Sindiru and Kogi were powerless to oppose the invaders.

Arabs in Sindiru (1885–1889)

The death of Lugör coincided with the coming of the Arabs to Sindiru in about 1885 to 1879, (Beaton, 1934; Spagnolo, 1933). Lado, the brother of Lugör and son of Pitya, also called *Lado Ngek* by his age mates, succeeded to the thankless task of defending the country from the Arab invaders.

Hitherto, the Arabs had contented themselves with Sindiru's subservience, but now they proceeded to hurry her. Sindiru's troubles were further exacerbated by a continued enmity and attacks from neighbouring chiefs. Lado finally fled the country to Fajulu country where he took refuge at mountain *Maribe'*. Spagnolo (1933: 279) refers to this period as the "Bari Dispersal", according to the Bari text, translated into English by Beaton. The text reads:[45]

"In the days of old, men were very numerous, and their herds were countless, but there came a time when the Turk descended on the land, and swept away youths, girls and cattle so that the land was desolate. The survivors, who had fled at once, and whom the Turks had not carried off, scattered to the north and, in fact, penetrated to Pajok, while some reached Palabek of Oli, some Ma'di Lokung, and others Paloro of Lokung" (Spagnolo 1933:279).

When they had remained there some years, the villages of the Acholi and Ma'di grievously wronged them; if a man had previously gone with a wife or daughters, all these were taken by force and he was left alone in the world. When the Bari saw the treatment that was being meted out to them, they held secret conclaves, and told their women, who had all been taken by force to escape at night. At the appointed night, they all collected in one place, and secretly fled to Bari country. However, they did not all come because some had not received the message. When they afterwards heard it, they were eager to escape in secret; but the Böri (Acholi) proved cunning and, if any fugitive escaped in secret, someone ran after him along this road and they were all slain. When the land was so desolate, men could not find cattle for marriage and began to marry with spears and hoes. Again when the Bari began to increase, then the Lokoya (Oxoriok) came to trouble them with war and they were engaged in battle. Again the Bari quarrelled among themselves and the villages came into conflict; this village would invade that and those would invade others. When they had collected for a large dance to which they all came and danced by clans, they always fell to fighting. Thus it was that the Bari grew fewer and fewer."

Amid such circumstances, Lado fled.

Wani (1885-1897)

Lado's nephew, Wani the son of Lugör, became Rain Chief after Lado fled into exile at Maribe. He was also called Wani Yemba 'dija. Wani Yemba 'dija married Kiden the sister of Luala the Chief of the Lulubö. Wani had remained at Sindiru when Lado fled the country.

Now, Wani quarrelled with his brother-in-law Luala and was attacked by Luala's brother Pitya. Pitya called the army of Mödi Adum, the buccaneer from Gondokoro to his aid. The combined force of the alliance was too much for Wani and he fled north and took refuge with *Kirba,* the Chief of the village of *Logo,* who 'led out his forces against Pitya and slew him'. Luala was incensed with the death of his brother and again called on Mödi Adum's army for help.

In the counterattack that ensued Wani was killed in battle. The people of Sindiru, however, contend that Wani was captured alive but was murdered by Mödi in cold blood. They believed that Mödi had a motive for killing Wani because he was avenging the death of his brother-in-law. Although Mödi Adum was a Bari originally from Gondokoro, and in spite of the bitter enmity between the Bari and the Lulubö, Mödi could still take the side of the Lulubö because he was married to Suköji, the daughter of Chief Luala. Mödi Adum, a member of the Nyori 'Doggale clan, was propelled into prominence and instant riches with the coming of the Arabs to Gondokoro around 1859. When the Arab invaders first reached Gondokoro, Mödi Adum threw his lot with them. 'Owning rich herds and possessing a number of rifles presented to him by his Arab masters, he became a power in the land and sold his services to all who would employ him' (Beaton:180). He penetrated the Lulubö from whence he married the daughter of Luala. The Pager version of the story was that, indeed, Mödi had captured Wani alive and handed him over to the Lulubö who then killed him on their way home.

Loro Kimbo, the Rain Chief of Pipiri, was so impressed with Mödi's prowess that he invited him to become the Chief of Pager. Mödi was able to gather together the scattered people of Pager and made them one again.[46]

Meanwhile, Lugör had died in exile among the Fajulu. His death, however, coincided with the advance of the Belgian expedition under Chaltin to capture Rejaf. Leju fled back home only to find Wani already dead. He was at once recognized as Rain Chief. He was chief when Uganda Government took over the east bank of the Nile, all the way to Gondokoro.

From Leju (1897) to the time of Pitya-Lugör (1932), the glory of Sindiru had departed. The gifts of cattle that in the olden days used to pour in from the surrounding Bari villages, and as a far away as the Fajulu, the Nyangwara and the Mundari dried up. There was not a single cow to be found in all of Sindiru. In 1930 and 1931, the feud between Kogi and Sindiru rekindled.

From this time on, Sindiru ceased to be the seat of Rain-Making and the seat of political power in Bari land. Political power had shifted to Bilinyang/Gondokoro axis.

7

Bilinyang and Gondokoro (1765–1932)

While this was going on in the south, a lot was also happening further north of Sindiru, specially in Bilinyang and Gondokoro. We recall that Subek, the elder son of Jada at Sindiru, had left Sindiru and migrated north to where he took abode at Bilinyang soon after his father died. In order not to rival his younger brother Kose, who was by all accounts the better rain-maker, Subek decided to move north, looking for greener pastures. On arrival at Bilinyang, Subek took abode among the Pannyigilo, Lumbari and the Dung clans who asked him to be Rain Chief of the village. This was about from 1765 to 1785.

At that time, Loro 'Doggale, a *Panyingilotyo*, was Chief of Bilinyang. The Panyigilo clan was the *komonyekak* (the owners of the land) of both Bilinyang and Ilibari/Gondokoro. As luck would have it, Subek and his family were later on 'to hold the office of the Rain Chief and several of the minor posts as village Headmen. Traditions claim the following were the family of Loro 'Doggale at time of the coming of the Bekat to Bilinyang: 'Doggale, Loro, Bambo, Tongun. Tongun had two sons; Yugusuk and Lutor lo-Tongun.

Subek's coming to Bilinyang introduced social tension and eventually socio-political change in both Bilinyang and Ilibari. Hitherto, the Monyekak was the supreme authority in the land. With the coming of Subek and his alleged ability to make rain, the powers of the monyekak were soon usurped by the Rain Chief. Within a generation of Subek's arrival, the Rain Chief had eclipsed the original chief, the Monyekak. Although the *monyekak* had magical functions to fulfill at seedtime, at harvest and before a hunt, and still holds a position of sociological importance in the life of the village, most of the business of the village was now done by the Rain Chief.

The take-over was made the more easy because of the Bari belief that the Rain Chief possessed special powers. When offended, the Rain Chief had powers to unleash all sorts of woes on the offending party, ranging from floods, drought, locusts and pestilence. For example, he could punish the offending person or village by sending swarms of insects, diseases such as, *dyedyero* ('small or chicken-pox), famine, or cause general infertility in both men and women, or any such punishment as he chose. The Bari held the Rain Chief in absolute awe.

According to Spagnolo (1933:299), when the Rain Chief was invited to bless the seeds of the village on the onset of the rainy season, and this was done often, a large entourage accompanied him on such trips. He was then placed in the middle of the compound while seated on the thighs of an elderly woman of the village. This done, he was then anointed all over the body with oil while the women sang and danced. The Rain Chief would then convey his blessings to the seeds, the fields, the women and the land. When he had performed all these, the Chief would then be given cattle, goats and any other gift the people might offer. As is to be expected, these offerings made the Rain Chiefs comparatively wealthy. With this wealth, they were able to have more influence over the traditional chiefs (the land chiefs). With these riches, Subek, the foreigner from south, was able to eclipse 'Doggale', the Panyigilo traditional chief of Bilinyang and Gondokoro, quite easily.

It would appear that rainmaking was a new phenomenon in Bari society. As we have already alluded, the Monyekak predated the Matat Lo Piong (Spagnolo 1933:321). He was the one that held counsel in Bari land. He blessed the land and its people with the *Lori* (a special teethed and pointed iron spear). He interceded to God on behalf of the people whenever there was calamity in the land. He was the sole advisor. He did not heed advice from anybody and all and sundry had to listen and obey him.

The Monyekak authorized war and performed cleansing rituals after war. He named all the big trees, all the forests, bodies of water (*kö'buluwöt*), streams and rivers. He was not to be provoked because by doing so, one might cause him to bring pestilence on the land or prevent the rains from coming altogether. The powers of the aboriginal Monyekak and the Rain Chief caused a great deal of tension and at times civil strife. The intensity of the rivalry varied from one village to another and from time to time. It ended during colonialism.

First contact with outside world

Dere (about 1785–1805)

Take over of power from the Panyigillo by the Bekat at Bilinyang appeared to have been peaceful. When Subek died, he left his clan fully established at Bilinyang. His son Dere became Rain Chief after him. Dere was the second son of Subek. His elder brother, Tombe, opted out of the rainmaking business altogether and migrated further north to Mögiri, a village about nine miles east of Bilinyang. At Bilinyang, Muludyang assumed power from his father Dere and ruled up to 1825.

It was not until Logunu's time, about 1840, that momentous events would begin to shake Bari country and eventually irrevocably change the way of life of the Bari people. These events started with the coming of the first European to Bari land.

The first European

Chief Logunu (1840)

Werne d'Arnand led the first expedition sent by Mohammed Ali in 1840 to discover the source of the Nile. On April 28, 1841 a certain M. Thibault, a French traveller, wrote to the Société de Géographie de Paris from Khartoum describing an expedition of exploration which he had just accomplished up the White Nile on behalf of the Egyptian Government. Quoting from Beaton (1934:184–188), and because of its importance, the text is reproduced in full:

"My letter of last October has made you acquainted with what happened to me and with the dangers I have encountered on various travels into the interior of Africa, and above all on the one from which I returned on March 30, 1841, after an absence of five months. I undertook this journey up the White Nile, the sources of which, as yet unexplored, will always remain so, if expeditions of a similar importance or geographical study, continue to rely on military persons, by custom inclined to demonstrations of hostility. It is useless to recount afresh the troubles and obstacles I met with last year; this year's expedition, although more peaceable, has only gone to show how distant is the solution of this problem. On this last journey, from which I returned on April 18, 1841, I was accompanied by two fellow country men, of whom one spent his time in scientific observations, while the other, a much traveled young man, who has crossed America, has knowledge necessary for mapping the course of the river. His astronomical readings will without doubt yield results and he will be able to give some accurate information on the unknown tracts of the various countries we have traversed. For my own part I did nothing but glean information; nevertheless, the notes I have taken on the habits and customs of the different races I have visited, and the collections of articles that I have amassed, will be, I hope, of some interest.

The first expedition, which penetrated as far as 5° 47′ altitude, was forced to return, owing to the depth of water being insufficient for their vessels. Progress has been made this year as far as 4° 43′ latitude and about 29° longitude. As a result, those famous Mountains of the Moon, which were thought to form an impassable barrier below latitude 8 North, have disappeared at this point to give place to unhealthy marshes, effects of which the natives suffer from, judging by their ailing and puny constitutions; they came to us in crowds to implore our help for their ailments."

While traversing about 130 miles more than the previous year, Thibault reports, they had discovered certain healthy peoples, whose number and courage might have been a source of danger to them, considering their poor means of defence. They were, however, prudent and natives showed themselves generous, and small gifts they made them procured for them on their side a hospitality worthy of the 'natural man'. Thibault, observed that it was not their black soldiers nor their firearms, hitherto unknown to the natives, that could have cowed them, but it was their 'floating mountains and the men riding on the yardarms; these novelties kept them within the limits of deference'. Armed with spears, the iron heads of which measured thirty inches, with bows and quivers, each containing thirty poisoned arrows and always in numbers from six to eight thousand, the natives could have easily sunk their frail and ill-prepared vessels. Instead, the Bari brought the newcomers gifts; oxen, animals of all kinds and elephant tusks of excellent ivory to exchange for glass beads.

According to Thibault,

> "These numerous peoples are ruled by a Chief, who is dressed, and he wore a plain shirt of blue cotton, which came to him, so he said, from one of his friends in the neighboring hills, the inhabitants of which were represented as cannibals—a fact which was corroborated by the whole populace. Prince Lagone sic. Logunu presented himself on January 24, 1841 at our ships in a way too remarkable for me not to describe it to you. Let us imagine we are watching a man more civilised than his followers, all of whom were naked, and made a point of displaying their athletic and muscular bodies, several 6′ 7′ or 6′ 8′, high, with a corresponding breadth of shoulder and surprising vigor; they wore enormous armlets of ivory on both arms, while iron rings covered their limbs. Their only deformity, as with all the tribes in this part of Africa, is the excision of the four front teeth in the lower jaw.
>
> At length M. Lagone [Muludyang logunu] had his arrival announced by a countless gathering of people. The repeated cries of thirty of his wives were accompanied by the melodious music of drums and antelope horns; he spread out his arms like an eagle in full flight to draw attention to the large sleeves of his old shirt. His head was decorated with a headdress of ostrich feathers, the movements of which he could regulate to the best of the

attractive music. Some dances were performed and Prince Lagone [Logunu] danced with the rest. At length, drawing near our boats, he went aboard that of the Turkish officers with a confidence that appeared to surprise them. It gave me great pleasure to see this man and the custom of sucking the forefinger of each of our officers was a mark of honor I found most singular. He made us understand that he was most flattered by our presence and that he awaited our generosity in the bestowal of gifts. These were words which in no way pleased our men; but however that may be, some serge garments of red cloth were distributed to Lagone, to his brothers and his sons, some white, blue and red beads to cover their limbs, and to increase the attractive sound of their band we added a bell of twenty-five pound weight, the clashing of which greatly delighted him; in a sitting of some hours he repeatedly showed us respect according to his custom. After eating some dates which we carried with us, he found them so much to his taste that he asked for many more and carried them off with the stones and the carpet spread out to receive him. All these people are as a rule beggars. Glass beads, with their bright colour and fine polish, they prefer to delicate and varied clothes. The women go naked, but on special occasions they wear a tanned hide over their loins and underneath that a fringe of cotton thread rubbed with a red ochre, which imparts a colour to it; the warrior class make use of this mineral to colour their bodies and they take on the colour of lobsters. Let us return to the females, who, when young, are pretty and well made, with muscular bodies, large eyes, rather slender noses, but with meagre heads of hair; these girls are only clothed in a light cotton fringe, which is so supple that the shape of the whole body is easily discernible.

Well received by these tribes, whom our men called unbelievers and slaves, we continued our journey to contact with the ranges of hills we had described several days before. It was January 1, 1841, that we reached a point beyond which progress was impossible; reefs of sand and rocks strewn in the bed of the river and its shallowness, all constrained us to cease our exploration.

> We sighted the various mountains which could be seen on the horizon and twenty-eight slaves from our guns announced our departure to the neighbourhood. The Turks were pleased to return, but we Frenchmen regretted that we could go no further. Could it be that we were on the point of discovering the sources of this remarkable river? The mountains through which it flows so peacefully could have given us an answer. We shall never have it, not even the natives could tell us.
>
> The mountains which we are leaving are rich with iron ore; the native avails himself of this and manufactures his weapons from it and uses it to trade among the neighbouring hills. The nearest lie in the country of Lagone, which is called Ber Bari; good tracts of country lie in front of masses of rock, which would have been for us so many more obstacles to surmount. Cultivation among the Bers or Berrh actually Bari is extensive, and their principal crops are white grain, sesame and small beans. Their houses are thatched and protected them from heavy rains of the equatorial regions.
>
> The definite result we achieved was to determine the course followed by the White Nile as far as the point we reached. Geographers have always believed that it comes from the west. It is now established that it rises in the East and that its supposed confluence with the Niger could only occur if for part of its course it flowed the other way—a thing impossible to credit. If we had pushed on a far as the equator, to within 4°North of which we had penetrated, we should have solved without possibility of contradiction a problem which must be taken up afresh with renewed energy. It is only a European Power that can solve the problem."

This was the land and people that Mr. Thibault found before the onslaught of the Turkish and Arab slave raiders and the ill reputation attributed to them by Mr. Samuel Baker in his book "Ismalia": peaceful, hospitable, polite, healthy and numerous.

Subek (1850)

Nyiggilo succeeded his father Logunu, but his reign was marred by the great famine of 1855–59, which the Bari refer to as Lokotet. Nyiggilo was suspected to have withheld the rains despite the fact that he had been given lucrative gifts for his services. 'After blaming now the slave-traders, then the mission and even their own medicine –men, Nyiggilo was at last held guilty.'[47]

Noticing rising anger and hostility amongst his people at Bilinyang, Nyiggilo fled and became a forlorn fugitive for sometime until, at last, he found refuge at Ilibari/Gondokoro, where he remained in hiding with his relative Möidi, at Kujönok, a section of Ilibari, near Li'bu. He hoped to be able to get a boat to escape to Khartoum to save his life. This was not to be, however. Soon, a large band of warriors gathered from far and wide and from the surrounding villages and headed for Kujönök to demand the head of Nyiggilo. For the rains to come again, the land had to purged of the sins of Nyiggilo and for that, he had to die to placate the Rain gods. But once more, Nyiggilo escaped to Swökir, but here, the irate band of youths caught up with him. He was captured and brutally put to death.[48] Franz Morlang (1859), a missionary at Gondokoro at the time and quoted in Seligman (1934:475–476) and Beaton (1934:188–189), gives a gruelling eyewitness account of the death of Nyiggilo:

> "He was forced to flee from Belenyan (Bilinyang), where his cattle were stolen and his dwelling burnt down, and for some time wandered as a hunted fugitive, until at last he found shelter with his kinsman Medi Mödi near Gondokoro, where he hoped to wait for a boat and save his life by escaping to Khartoum. But a numerous band of armed youths, gathered from far and wide, came to Kudschenok Kujönök the home of Medi and boisterously demanded Nyiggilo, the rain-maker. He escaped again, but was found in the neighbouring village of Tschuekir Swökir, and was struck down with blows from clubs and four spear-thrusts. His belly was slit open, and he was left for the vultures. So died Nyiggilo, the great Nyiggila...After his death, all the cattle of his family and relatives were seized and driven

away. His old mother died of anxiety and grief, his wives and children fled, some here and some there."[49] Apparently this is the traditional punishment meted out to offending rain-chiefs who dare to hide the rain. Haddon reports that a rain-chief killed for hiding the rain is buried like a commoner. 'His corpse is dragged near to water, his face is smeared with mud from the river bank, his body slashed, and his stomach ripped open, and he is left to the birds and scavengers'. His old friends are however allowed to bury their dead but only after the payment of cattle as ransom. 'He is then buried like a commoner, the apertures and cuts being left open'.

Lako (about 1870)

When Lako succeeded his father Subek as Chief, Bilinyang was already annexed to Turko-Egyptian Sudan and Gordon was governor of Equatoria after having taken over from Samuel Baker. With Bilinyang still being technically at war with the occupying forces at Gondokoro, Lako did not hesitate to ambush and eliminate two patrols sent out by Emin Pasha. Emin was enraged with the loss but there was not much he could do about it. The only thing he could do was to bid for time which came one cattle auction day at Li'bu, by the river bank. Emin had just returned from a pillaging raid from the Lutoho country with a drove of Lutoho cattle. Unaware of the mortal danger that his life was in, Lako rushed to the auction site in the hope of acquiring cheap cattle. Unfortunately for him, his presence was betrayed. He was captured and Emin Pasha had him behead.[50]

Another important Chief at Bilinyang after Lako was Lado-lo-Ide, who was chief from about 1885. Lado-lo-Ide was the son of Ide, the wife of Chief Logunu, who was inherited by his son Subek after his death. Subek begot Lado. He was Chief of Bilinyang during the time of the Mahdi's rebellion and contemporary of Lugör, Chief at Sindiru whom he supported in his failed attack against Köri, Chief of Kogi.

During Lado's reign, there was a split at Bilinyang caused by rivalry over rain Chieftainship. At that time, there were two Rain

Chiefs acting at the same time after the early death of Basan who was Rain Chief, leaving his young sons. Bilinyang was divided into two sections: the western section called *Indöru* was under Lado, the eastern part known as *Gitong* was the province of *Bepo-lo-Nyiggilo*. Bepo was old and weak when the Dervishes came. He made peace with them and was left in peace. Lado, however, was not so accommodating. He decided to challenge the invaders but owing to superior arms of the Dervishes, Lado lost most of his men. His home was razed to the ground and he temporarily surrendered. In due course, however, Lado was able to reconstitute the remnants of his forces and instead of waging war against the Dervishes, descended on *Gitong*, which he sacked, killing Bepo-lo-Nyiggilo in the struggle.

Lado did not rule a reunified Bilinyang for long, for fearing that he might foment more trouble for them, the Dervishes had him put under arrest at Rejaf for some time. He met his end at unexpected quarters— his in-law's at Wanyang in Mundari country. Lado was married at Wanyang and had some cattle there. After his release from prison, he headed for Wanyang to collect his cattle. It was during this visit that the inhabitants fell on him and murdered him. After Lado there was a line of inconsequential Rain Chiefs from Suke Lako (about 1890) Bambo Lako (1900), to Molodiang Logunu (1928) From Muludiang and Logunu's time, about 1914, to Ali Nyiggilo's time nicknamed Ali Bey Pitya's time, from about 1900 to 1932, the importance of the Rain Chief declined. There were now appointed chiefs, derisively called government chiefs.

8

The Coming of the Foreigners (1839–1883)

In spite of their wars with the Oxoriok, the Bari people were generally peaceful and prosperous before the coming of the invaders.

In 1839, a flotilla sent by Muhammed Emin Pasha succeeded in getting through the sudd and into Bari country *en route* to opening a route to Lake Albert in their quest for the search of the source of the Nile. That date marks the darkest day in Bari history. In the wake of the Pasha's flotilla, followed a chain of intruders: (a) government men, (b) ivory traders, (c) missionaries. Each group had its own agenda and intensely distrusted one another. Often, they were more than willing to incite local prejudices among the people in order to cause intertribal wars. All shared 'a common contempt for the southerner as an inferior being'.[51]

However, before the country and its people were destroyed, the foreigners who visited Bari country generally had a positive impression about the country and its people. For example, Werne, a member of the first expedition of Europeans to visit the Bari between 1841–1844, observed that on average, the heights of his hosts were 6.5 to 7 feet tall. He was very impressed with their 'classical features' which reminded him of Roman aristocrats and Egyptians murals and made him think that the Bari constituted the "protoplasm of the black race".[52] Like Werne before him, Lafargue (1845:159–160) could not help but declare in utter astonishment that the Bari were "the most beautiful human race that exists on the face of the earth". Hartmanns (1884:129) in his turn suggested "that the Bari might very well provide us with a model of the authentic 'noble savage'.

The arrival of the white people following the Nile predicted by Lokuryeje, the famous *'bunit*, became true one gloomy day in 1839. It all began with the arrival of the first flotilla of Muhammed Ali Pasha in 1839.

At the turn of the 19th century, the search for the sources of the Nile, the quest for new territories and wealth brought a wave of rapacious and murderous hordes of vandals to Bariland. The contact between the Bari people and the scheming foreigners was to lead by the end of the twentieth century to the total destruction of the Bari people and their way of life.

First, came the explorers, followed predictably by the missionaries on a proselytizing mission to win more benighted souls to the lord. Then they were fallowed by the Turks, the Arabs, the British, the Belgians and an assortment of other unsavory breed of cut-throats. These invasions were arguably the bloodiest in Africa's colonial history. This period is the worst in Bari history and admittedly, southern Sudan. It saw the near total destruction of the Bari as a people. Not only did they lose all their cattle to plunder, but also, the land was emptied of nearly all its able-bodied population. By the time the excesses of these committed despoilers were brought to an end, the Bari nation had been reduced to a smoldering, bleeding, dismal wasteland peopled by remnants of an impoverished, disparate, and traumatized groups of malnourished inhabitants.

Thousands of young men and women were carried off into slavery and many more died due to famine, especially the famous five years' famine from 1874 to 1879 and what the Bari still remember as *'Lokotet'* and diseases. Although the Bari valiantly resisted the long and protracted pillaging of their country for over a century, the force of superior arms finally prevailed.

When stability was finally established in the early part of the twentieth century, Bari society had changed beyond recognition. The millions of cattle that used to loll and graze peacefully in the mead were no more. Gone also were the endless populous villages; from Bilinyang and Mögiri in the east to Nyrökönyi in the west and from Mogolla to Bedden in the south. The Dervishes descended on Bilinyang and Mögiri-two large Bari villages East of the present town of Juba) —raiding and plundering. A few years later, Arabi Daffaalla (a very notorious Arab slave trader known throughout Bari country for his brutality) plundered Bari country more thoroughly than before. He even stole the rifle of Wani Lokose (the chief of Bilinyang) given to him by Ali Bey (one of the lieutenants of Amin Pasha the governor of Equatoria at the time).

The loss of livelihood and a greater part of its population triggered a drastic socio-economic change in Bari society. The stark distinction that marked the social classes ceased or was greatly relaxed. Everybody was equally impoverished and all classes could now own cattle. Some of the lower classes became even richer than the lui. When the Bari lost all their cattle, it also implicitly meant that the lui, the upper class of Bari society also lost the cornerstone of their power.

The foreigners who had come to Bari country needed ivory. At first, these were in plenty and were controlled by the *lui* who sold it to the ivory traders. As the number of ivory traders increased, the amount of ivory decreased, until it was finally exhausted. Now, the *yari*, who were professional elephant hunters any way, were the best placed to benefit from the trade and could provide that commodity. They became very wealthy. The introduction of cash economy in the early part of the 20th century was another added factor that helped free the lower classes. The blacksmiths too began to earn money and prosper. In the olden days, hoes, trinkets and so on were purchased with milk. With nearly all the cattle gone, milk became scarce, instead *dura* (some sort of grain) and honey was given in exchange. What was most important in the change brought about by these vicissitudes was that the servile classes became independent in their marriage arrangements and other material needs. They were now able to marry independently from their chiefs and therefore owed them nothing. Instead of paying bride price in cattle as they used to, the Bari now gave goats and hoes. While in the old days cattle was owned by prominent freemen, now all classes owned cattle. Because of this, even the *'dupi* could now marry from the freemen.

Figure 6: *An illustration of Bari homestead*

This fact nullified the chief's claim on services and unquestioned loyalty. The chief's only claim on them was now based only on traditional right. The *'dupi*, because they had very little other than their services to offer, were not so lucky. Only a few of them managed to emancipate themselves through hard work. Until recently, the *'dupi* still cooked for the freemen during ceremonies.

Thus, it can clearly be seen that the loss of the basic means of livelihood cattle and destruction of the population led to a radically changed social structure, social relations and cultural practices among the Bari society. For example, the *kurum*i (the forest cattle enclosure) and the culture associated with it is now lost forever. Gone are also the rituals of the rites of passage such as the age set groups- the *b*e*r*.

The dislocation of the pastoral way of life of the Bari led to the adoption of a new way of life, from a pastoralist, to agro-pastoralist mode of existence. The young men and young women, who were in the past occupied with the cattle, now joined the older men in the fields.

The first Bari the foreigners met at Li'bu was a man called Swaka who was alleged to have been the chief of Gondokoro. It was one of these who first saw the foreigners. This is a version of a native story:

> "Upon the arrival of the *gela* (foreigners) here among us they found a certain man at the landing place upon the river, called Lokoya. And they spoke and said: 'Lokoya, thou art chief.' And Lokoya said: 'Alas, and how can I become chief? Because I am a *tumunit* and my work is upon the river.' And they said: 'You be so.' And Lokoya said: 'Yes,' but he answered vainly, i.e. for the sake of answering. And *Mödi-lo-Busuk* was chief of the *Panygilo*, also he was *monyekak*. And another man, too, was a big man; his name was Loro lo Yiro. And Lokoya told him, saying: 'Verily, those strangers seized me at the landing place, saying I was chief, and I said: 'Alas, it is truly not possible because I have my chief over there in Ilibari (the district of Gondokoro) on the further bank." And Loro lo Yiro sadi: 'Yes, Lokoya.' And forthwith he beat the drum which went *kir, kir, kir*. And then the whole of Ilibari gathered together at the house of Lako lo Yiro, and said: What is the matter, chief?' And he said: 'Verily, Lokoya says the *gela* have found him upon the landing place over there, and they made him chief, and he refused, therefore he has come here.' And those people said: 'How is this thing to be?' And Loro lo Yiro said: 'Ask the chief, Mödi lo Busuk,' because Mödi was the great chief of the Panyigilo, and also was monyekak. And Mödi said: 'Loro thou art to be chief.' And Loro that it was that became chief."[53]

The first real contact of the Bari with the foreigners from the north was on January 19, 1841, when Mohamed Ali the viceroy of Egypt sent the second expedition to discover the source of the White Nile. It was a peaceful, in fact, festive encounter for the Bari. The German geographer Werne who accompanied the expedition described their reception as 'triumphant procession'.

On both banks the boasts were followed by singing and dancing crowds. Glass beads were traded for cows, spears and ornaments

---

...ggilo, who understood Arabic and the way a gun worked, ...g the welcoming crowd. When he heard Vaudey shout ...npowder was finished he opened the counterattack and ...he soldiers killed.

...et his fate while trying to escape by swimming across the ...was killed by Mödi, the Master of the land in the part of ...a relative of Nyiggilo. Matat killed matat, a proper match ...to local ethics and warfare".[55]

...barely eleven years after the arrival of the traders, Bari ...was in flames and total chaos. One year after the fight at ...t resulted in the death of Vaudey, another calamity struck ...a great drought set in that lasted four long years, from ...1860, Lejean (1865: 74). It is still remembered in these ...Bariland.

...ught was particularly disastrous for Gondokoro and ...g:

...d bodies everywhere, mothers who threw their babies ...m they could no longer feed into the Nile and vain ...npts of chieftains of Ilibari to stop wide-spread robbery ...violence by summery execution (Morlang 1862/63:115).

...e of the drought, violence became rampant in Bariland. ...y, burglaries and homicide became common (Faufmann ...80). Writing about the famine, Morlang (1862:82), one of ...ssionaries who witnessed the famine, painted a very bleak ...pressing picture of the situation. The effects of the famine ...ch that when it ended:

...Gondokoro itself, only three houses were left. But, before ...onset of the drought, all accounts of the travelers who ...me to Bari country speak of numerous villages and dense ...pulation. Fr. Angelo Vinco, who frequently moved from ...ndokoro to Bilinyang, speaks of Marju and Bilinyang as ...rming one continuous series of settlements" (Morlang ...62:82).

while the boats moved on slowly. Chief Logunu, who was chief of both Gondokoro and Bilinyang, received the travellers. Logunu made a very impressive impression on the visitors and was given a big bronze cowbell.

After his death, his sons Subek-Lo-Logunu and Nyiggilo-lo-Logunu emerged as rivalling leaders of the Bari. Nyiggilo was sired by Logunu from a wife he inherited from his father. He was therefore, according to Bari custom, the brother, and not the son of Logunu. Nyiggilo struck up friendship with the ivory trader Brun-Rollet who took him to Khartoum in 1844 at his own request but escaped very narrowly from being enslaved.[54] When he finally returned from Khartoum, Nyiggilo, as he predicted, acquired a key position in the trade of goods from Khartoum with the eastern hinterland of Bilinyang and travelled widely to Pari, Loudo and Lotuho. 'He was also the local protector of the Austrian missionaries who ran the mission post in Gondokoro from 1852 to 1860' (Brun-Rollet 1885:188).

Nyiggilo established close friendship with the missionary Fr. Angelo Vinco who used to accompany him on his trading expeditions. Fr. Vinco is said to have acquired the status of a jwök, a divine spirit among the people. As such, he played an important role of peacemaker within Bari society in both internal as well as external conflicts. On one occasion, he reconciled the Bari and Pari. In another, he averted imminent war between the Bari and an alliance of Liria, and three other Lokoya villages force against the Bari.

Civil war at Gondokoro

Missionary vs slave-traders

By the mid 1840s, two groups had firmly established their presence at Gondokoro; the missionaries and the traders from Khartoum. Soon these two groups were at each other's throats, drawing the local people into the feud. While the traders indulged in the slave trade and found a willing ally in Subek-lo-Logunu, the other faction opposed slavery and was led by chief Nyiggilo and his friend the trader Brun-Rollet who was prepar[ing] international pressure against slavery.

This division was unfortunate. It unv[eiled to the] Arab slave armies an opportunity to c[apitalize on] their differences. The wars that brok[e out gave] traders a golden chance to capture [slaves.] According to Brun-Rollet, by the midd[le of 1850s,] trader armies had formed and, were nov[v fomenting] wars between Bari chieftains. They glad[ly captured and] promptly sold them off as slaves on the s[lave markets.]

By 1852, there was now open war bet[ween the two] factions. The foreigners on the opposin[g sides were] Vinco and the mission who supported [Nyiggilo, and those] who supported Subek and the Arab slave [traders, led by] the Vice-Consul of Sardinia. The bitter riv[alry, which] was to lead to the premature death of Fr. V[inco, was] caused by the continuous harassment and [attacks by] the slave traders and their Bari allies'[...] According to Brun-Rollet, Vinco was accor[ded honours.] The anti-slavery priest was buried in the mi[dst] of Ilibari. Over '3000 to 4000 people came [and] eight days of mourning were observed' (Bru[n-Rollet).]

Two years latter, on April 4, 1854 at Li'bu, [Vinco met his] death at the hands of Mödi, the chief of Ili[bari. According to] Brun-Rollet again, this was how he met his de[ath:]

"A crowd of over 5000 Bari had gathered [at the] river near the Mission Station to w[elcome] Knoblecher who had just arrived from Khar[toum. A boat] of Vaudey's trading firm happened to pass [by on] its way from Rejaf to Li'bu. Mohamed Eff[endi] fired a salute in honour of the Pro-Vicar, w[hich] killed a Bari boy in the waiting crowd and h[it another in] the leg. The Bari immediately reacted by sh[ooting at] the ship. To this, Mohamed Effendi respond[ed by firing at] the crowd. Vaudey who was in Ligbu imme[diately came to] Mohamed Effendi's aid, taking fifteen sol[diers and] chasing anybody in his way by gunfire".

The severe drought and the famine were attributed to many causes, chief among which was chief Nyiggilo, who also doubled as the Rain Chief of the area. Frustration and general anger among the Bari reached such a pitch by June 21, 1859 that they felt that the only way to cure the curse was to put Nyiggilo to death.

Unfortunately, the death of Chief Nyiggilo, far from bringing to an end the melee in the land, heralded in more troubles for the beleaguered nation. Nyiggilo's death ushered in a breed of rapacious ruffians—the turjuma, cargo chiefs and government men, intermediaries and a horde of all sorts of carpetbaggers in the service of the foreigner. It also marked the end of the role of the traditional Rain Chief and the chief of the land. These new type of vigorous barbarians would henceforth continue to control the affairs of the nation for nearly the next three decades.

9

Trader-Chiefs (1859–1885)

Throughout the 1850s, trade in ivory with the Bari and Bari hinterland expanded. For example, according to Gray (1961:131), in 1851 alone, twelve boats left Khartoum for the ivory trade on the White Nile. In 1856, there were forty boats. The number of boats increased to eighty boats by 1859. The dominant forces in Bariland from 1860 to 1871 were the Christian missionaries and the Egyptian trading firm of Al Aqqad, locally managed by a certain nefarious Abu Sa'ud, an Egyptian of Kurdish-Turkish descent.

Al Aqqad was one of the trading companies established by the Egyptian government purportedly to conduct legitimate ivory trade on the White Nile. The owners of the company were for the most part, Arab and subjects of the Egyptian government:[56]

> "Who had deserted their agricultural occupations in the Sudan and had formed companies of brigands in the pay of the various merchants of Khartoum. The largest trader had about 2,500 Arabs in his pay, employed as pirates or brigands, in Central Africa. These men were organized after a rude military fashion, and armed with muskets; they were divided into companies, and were officered in many cases by soldiers who had deserted from their regiments in Egypt or the Sudan".

Baker (1871) noted that each trader occupied a special district where, by a division of his forces in a chain of stations each of which represented 300 men, he could exercise a right of possession over a certain amount of territory. Through this means and under the guise of legitimate commerce, large tracts of the southern Sudan was parcelled out to the bands of marauding armed bandits of Arab slave traders from Khartoum. Often they made alliances with the native tribes to attack and destroy their neighbours, and to carry off their women and children, together with vast herds of sheep and cattle.

At first, things went fairly well. The Bari were friendly and had plenty of stock of ivory to sell to the annual government convoys from Khartoum. As word spread among the traders, many flocked to Bariland to get a share of the trade. By 1850, the stock of ivory had run out. Now, instead of the traders waiting for the Bari hunters to bring in the ivory, they themselves took to hunting for the elephants. The price of ivory rose. Rival firms set up their own supply units, leaving a garrison to collect ivory between seasons and live off the country as best or worst as they might. As the trade in ivory increased, so did competition between rival trading houses operating in Bariland. Many local chiefs became intermediaries for the traders in the collection of ivory from the hinterland and the distribution of goods from the traders to the hinterland. The entrance of many traders into the ivory trade resulted in a scarcity of the commodity and exacerbation of competition.

With the depletion of elephant herds and scarcity of ivory, slave hunting soon became the main source of revenue. The bands of ivory traders and elephant hunters rapidly transformed themselves into marauding and rapacious terror gangs of human hunters, pillaging the countryside mercilessly for cattle and capturing men, women and children for slaves. The Arab slavers soon turned the places they controlled in Bariland into perfect hell on earth. At Gondokoro, for example, they made it their special pastime of feeding Bari captives to crocodiles at Li'bu as a way of encouraging them to reveal where the people were hiding.

> "At that time, the Bari used to hide women, old men and children far away from home as a protection against surprise night slave raids by the Ansars and Turks. People did not keep grain and other foods in the granary because the slave traders would either steal or burn it. Grain was buried deep in the ground."[57]

According to Moorhead (1910:78), Khartoum in the eighteen-sixties was as strange and wild as Zanzibar; indeed the two towns between them drained off the great bulk of the slave and ivory trade of East Africa, all the caravans south of the Equator going out south-eastwards to the Indian Ocean and those to the north descending the Nile to Khartoum. In those days, the Egyptian ruled, actually pillaged is the word, from Khartoum. 'Practically every official from the Governor-general, Musa Pasha, downwards was involved in some way in the slave-trade, and the garrison of fifteen thousand Egyptian and Nubian troops lived on the land as an army of occupation might live, except that it was far more ruthless and disorderly', (Moorhead 1910:78). The business of the so called government was to extort taxes from the natives either by the use of the whip, or armed raids on the cattle and the grain stores in the villages. The practice was such that any penniless Arab adventurer could become rich overnight. All he needed to do was borrow money at a hefty interest of eighty two percent and set off on an expedition down south to capture slaves to sell.

The practice had been that a Khartoum slave trader would sail from Khartoum to the south with a force of about two or three hundred armed Arab men, and would after reaching a chosen area, disembark and immediately seek for an alliance with a willing native chieftain. Then together, the tribesman and the Khartoum slavers would launch a surprise attack on some unsuspecting neighbouring village in the night, firing the huts just before dawn and shooting indiscriminately into the flames. Of those who survived the conflagration, the women were the most coveted booty. Upon capture, these women were secured in a special manner. The standard way had been to place a heavy forked pole, known as *sheba,* on their shoulders, while the heads were locked in by a cross-bar and the hands tied to the pole in front.

If children were also captured in the raid, they were bound to their mothers' backs and also by a chain that passed round their necks. Nothing was left behind. 'Everything the village contained would be looted—cattle, ivory, grain, even the crude jewellery that was cut off the dead victims (Moorhead 1910:81). Duplicity was not uncommon. Stories are told that often, the trader would turn against his native ally and despoil him in the same way he had done to others. Generally, however, these unholy alliances were kept for long; the native chieftain was allowed to build up fresh stores of slaves and ivory while the trader was disposing of the last consignment at Khartoum. 'Every trader had his own territory and by mutual agreement the country was parcelled out all the way from Khartoum to Gondokoro and beyond' (Moorhead 1910).

Moorhead (1910:81) points out that in a good season, a 'slaver in a small way could get 20,000 lb. of good ivory worth £4,000 in Khartoum, plus 400 or 500 slaves worth £5 or £6 each-a total of perhaps £6,5000. With this capital, the trader can pay off his debts and year by year, expand his businesses. He noted that, 'nothing more monstrous or cruel than this traffic had happened in history, 'for it was more highly organized than the slaving in Tanganyika'.

Such was the situation in most of the southern Sudan, including the Nuba Mountains. By the time Baker hoisted the Egyptian flag near the old location of the mission at Li'bu, most of the Bariland was under the control of Abu S'aud of Al Aqqad and Company, and his local collaborators. Abu Sa'ud, the Egyptian employed Kurd, had two trading posts, one at Gondokoro on the east bank and the other at Rejaf on the west bank of the Nile. He had other slave stations further inland, all the way from Liria to Lotuho land. His agent at Gondokoro was Loro-lo-Lako, still known in Gondokoro to this day as Loro-lo Jurön, "a commoner, who had started as a *turjuman*, (an interpreter) and middleman assisting the traders." At Rejaf, Lako-lo-Rondyang, nicknamed *Abu Kuka* (possessor of an enlarged scrotum) was the intermediary. Strangely, although the two men collaborated fully with the traders in the enslavement of their own people, they were nonetheless vehemently opposed to the establishment of an Egyptian state and the presence of missionaries in Bariland.

The persistent attacks on the mission led by the two men, especially Loro-lo-Lako, led to the closure of the Catholic mission at Gondokoro in 1860. Beltrame (1881:312) laments that in a period of twelve years paid for with the lives of twelve missionaries, the missions were only able to convert 47 Baris to Christianity.

Samuel Baker (1869–1876)

With pressure mounting on the Egyptian government "to suppress the slave-hunters of Central Africa and to annex the countries constituting the Nile Basin, with the object of opening those savage regions to legitimate commerce and establishing a permanent government", Samuel W. Baker was dispatched to end the slave trade by the Khedive of Egypt. He arrived in Gondokoro on April 15, 1871, exactly forty two years after the visit of the first European to Bariland and immediately Christianed Gondokoro "Ismalia" in honour of his employer, Khedive Ismail. Compared with his first visit to the southern Sudan in 1860, Baker would say that what he now saw after his return saddened him greatly:[58]

> "The country is sadly changed; formerly, pretty native villages in great numbers were dotted over the landscape, beneath the shady clumps of trees, and the land was thickly populated. Now, all is desolate: not a village exists on the mainland; they have all been destroyed, and the inhabitants have been driven for refuge on the numerous islands of the river; these are thronged with villages, and the people are busily cultivating the soil."

Unfortunately, Baker's coming to Bariland was yet another sad, bloody and unhappy chapter in Bari history. Although he had come with good intention to rescue the natives from the ravages of the slave trade, he found much to his disappointment, that the whole Bari nation was in a hostile and an unwelcoming mood, thanks to the activities of the slave traders. The Bari, believing him to be yet again one of the conniving foreigners, refused to welcome and cooperate with him. The Bari did not only refuse to welcome Baker, they also refused to give him food and cooperate in building his camp. They had had far too many unhappy experiences with Arabs and Europeans to trust another one of them.

Tragically, for both the Bari and Baker, Baker misunderstood this mood. Instead, he took a personal offence. He was particularly incensed with the fact that the Bari would neither give him grain nor sell him cattle to feed his hungry troops. A further tragic misunderstanding was a cultural one. Baker did not know that the Bari together with other cattle keeping peoples do not as a rule sell their cattle, either to a Bari or any other person. Instead of persuading the Bari, he resorted to the use of force to secure food for his starving soldiers. Raiding Bari cattle and other animals, including grain, became his main means of acquiring supplies for his troops. That was a fatal mistake. The action not only helped to alienate him completely from the people but also destroyed whatever good will there ever was. From then on, the Bari treated and regarded Baker, just as another cattle thief. And Baker in his turn, would consider the Bari as good for nothing warlike vermins.

By 1873, there was open war between Baker and the Bari. Lako-lo-Rondyang of Tokiman and Loro-lo-Lako from Gondokoro backed by Abu S'aud led the Bari resistance against Baker and by implication, the establishment of an Egyptian state in Bariland. Bilinyang, whose chief Bepo-lo Nyiggilo was an in-law and ally of Loro-lo-Lako, also joined the war against Baker. All the anti-occupation forces helped by Lokoya allies mounted protracted raids on the camp of the Egyptian governor at Li'bu at Gondokoro.

It was an uneven fight; bows and arrows against machines guns and canons. The Bari warriors of the combined villages of Gondokoro, under Loro-lo-Lako, Bilinyang, supported by Lokoya warriors under the command of Bepo-lo-Nyiggilo, and Tokiman, under Lako-lo-Rondyang were no match for the "forty thieves" of Baker. Bari resistance ended with the siege of Bilinyang on August 30, 1871 which lasted thirty-five days. Of the siege itself, Baker wrote the following in his diary:[59]

"On August 30, 1871, I started with a force of 450 men, one gun, and one rocket-trough for Hale's three-pounder rockets. ...The Bari of Belian sic Bilinyang Mountain were well provided with guns and ammunitions, which they had in various massacres of the slave-traders' parties some years before. One occasion they had killed 126 of the traders in one day, and had possessed themselves of their arms, with many cases of cartridges. On several occasions, they had destroyed smaller parties with the same result and they had never been at peace with Abou Saood Abu S'aud since he had treacherously murdered their sheik chief and his family. Recently, having allied with Abou Saood's friends (the Bari of Gondokoro) against the government, some of the Belian people had ventured to trade, and had established a communication with Abou Saood's people, from whom they purchased ammunition in exchange for tobacco."

Baker's counter-offensive against the triple alliance of Loro, Bepo and Abu Sa'ud was a siege of Bilinyang, which lasted thirty-five days. When it was finally over, the whole of Bilinyang lay in total ruin, all the crops were either looted or destroyed and cattle stolen by Baker's hungry troops. In any case, the whole purpose of the siege of Bilinyang was to secure grain and meat for his troops at Gondokoro.

Baker wrote in his diary that he had information that the villages of Bilinyang and the islands south of Rejaf, about fourteen miles south of Gondokoro, were teeming with corn for the taking. Acquisition of that grain would make him independent of corn from Khartoum. The grain and cattle taken in the raid on Bilinyang was not enough to feed Baker's troops. Further raids were necessary to procure food for the troops. Procuring food by force for his soldiers became Baker's main means of provisioning his troops in Bariland. Not only did the Bari lose their best men in the battles of resistance that ensued, they also lost millions of their herds and main source of livelihood. In later years, the practice of raiding for Bari cattle and grain, termed *ghazwe,* would become the official manner of provisioning government garrisons in Equatoria. Subsequent invaders would even follow this method of acquiring provisions for troops more ruthlessly: the Egyptians, the Mahdists and Belgians. Baker claimed that he could not find a peaceful solution to the problem to procuring food for his troops. But by resorting to raiding for provisions in order to feed his troops, 'Baker set the pattern for future relations between subsequent governments whether Egyptian, Mahdist or Belgian and the surrounding villages.'[60]

After thoroughly looting Bilinyang, Baker's next targets were the populous areas south of Gondokoro along the Nile, namely: Rejaf and Beden. With the defeat of the people of Rejaf and Beden, Loro-lo-Lako at Gondokoro could not continue with the resistance on his own. He surrendered. With Loro's surrender, Baker considered the pacification of Bariland complete.

However, Baker's activities and excesses had begun to cause concern in some western capitals and he was finally forced to withdraw from Bariland. Instead of coming as a saviour to stop the misery caused by the slave trade, Baker ended up causing more widespread destruction and loss of life in Bariland than had ever been witnessed before. By the time he was asked to withdraw, Baker had become apathetic about the whole business of ending the slave trade. He wrote:

> "However much we may condemn the horrible system of slavery, the results of emancipation have proved that the negro does not appreciate the blessings of freedom, nor does he show the slightest feelings of gratitude to the hand that broke the rivets of his fetters."[61]

But, this is odd, if not unfair. Baker had just captured some slave boats carrying about one hundred and fifty women and children stowed away in a very small area at Fashoda and had the governor of the area free the captured slaves. He reports that, '...as the truth flashed across their delighted minds, they rushed upon me in a body, and before I had time for self-defence, I found myself in the arms of a naked beauty who kissed me almost to suffocation, and with a most unpleasant embrace, licked my eyes with her tongue' (Baker). This very embarrassingly emotional reaction can hardly be described as the behaviour of an ungrateful and a people unappreciative of freedom or a good act.

Although, Baker was asked to leave Bariland and Equatoria generally, the Khedive was not done with Equatoria yet. His spendthrift ways had sunk Egypt in more debt and he needed more money. He needed another European to carry on his imperial designs in Equatoria and the regions around the sources of the Nile. His choice fell on General Gordon.

General Gordon (1877–1880)

Gordon was 41 and already famous. He had served in the British army and fought in the Crimean War and China. Gordon took up appointment with the Khedive on January 28, 1874. His assignment was to establish a chain of military stations down the White Nile from Gondokoro to the source of the river in Buganda, to annex Buganda itself and toughen to launch Baker's steamers upon Lake Albert and Lake Victoria.[62]

General Gordon arrived to assume his post a year after Baker had left Equatoria. The province had gone to ruin. At Gondokoro, the garrison had lost all discipline. There was general mayhem. The old corrupt practice of the Egyptian officials was again in force.

Within five days, Gordon had put some order in place in Gondokoro; the officials dealing in the slave trade were dismissed and he dispatched some officials to make contact with Buganda. He immediately left for Khartoum to demand that henceforth, Equatoria be 'separated from the rest of the Sudan and treated as an independent state' (Moorhead 1910:159). Consent was granted by the Khedive although Ismail Pasha Ayoub, the governor-general, did not consent.

Back in Equatoria, he immediately moved the government station from Gondokoro to Rejaf, further south. Aware that the causes of Baker's troubles originated from the traders and their allies, Gordon sought to break the stranglehold the traders and the chiefs had on the people by breaking the chain in the provision of goods and services. Accordingly, he established a market at Rejaf and introduced money as a means of exchange. These moves were openly resisted by chief Lako-lo-Rondyang "Abu Kuka". He stood against Gordon's policy of establishing a market at Rejaf. Hitherto, all goods, whether brought in by steamers from Khartoum or extorted through *ghawe*, were conduited through chiefs who acted as middlemen and who would receive these textiles and beads in return, which they could distribute at their own discretion. Gordon opened a local market, introduced copper coins, and wage-labour (half a piaster per day for work at the station instead of payment in trade goods) as an alternative to raids.

Not drawing a lesson from Baker, Gordon made a mistake of making the wily slave trader Abu Sa'ud his second in command. Not happy with Gordon's presence in the area, he sought to undermine his authority and get him expelled from Rejaf. He accordingly instigated Lako-lo-Rondyang to close down the market using a band of Bari warriors. Learning from the woes of Baker, Gordon chose not to use force to put down the rebellion. Instead, he retaliated by exiling Lako-lo-Rondyang to Khartoum, 'to impress him with the power Gordon represented' (Douin, 1936:82–3). Lako returned from his exile as a loyal subject of the Egyptian government and a Moslem convert. This mode of punishment would become the norm for recalcitrant and errant chiefs.

Even with the deportation of Lako-lo-Rondyang to Khartoum, resistance to the Egyptian occupation was not over. For example, further south close to the Umö River, a collusion of six Rainmakers from Karpeto and Uma River, Kellang, Nyongkir, Gwodiang, Muggu-Jöndöru or Nyarbanga, Nyangwara, Muggi-Remonyo and Gumösi - had formed under the leadership of Moyok, a reputed *juök* (a person with thaumaturgical powers). These allied forces put up a stiff fight in defence of the area they controlled.

In 1874, these forces attacked reinforcements from Khartoum that were sent to Baker in the Acholi area, killing 28 soldiers. Similarly, one year later, in 1875, Moyok's forces attacked the forces under Gordon inflicting heavy casualties. Gordon, forces suffered heavy losses while the boat he was trying to pull upstream to Lake Albert ran aground near Muggi. "Two more expeditions were necessary to break the resistance and to declare the Bari pacified".[63]

When the pacification of the Bari ended, the government had six stations in Bariland stationed at: Gondokoro and Rejaf, opened by Baker; Lado to the north used as the capital of Equatoria Province from 1875–1885, and (the Lado Enclave from 1897 to 1906, Bedden, south of Rejaf, Kiri and Muggi further south on the Nile bank, opened by Gordon. Now each of these virtual garrison stations was manned by a huge army that depended for its livelihood on the surrounding countryside through plunder. For example, from 1884 to 1888, what others have rightly called 'the period of disintegration of Equatoria Province' during the Mahdiyya (188–1897) and the days of the Lado Enclave (1887–1906) plunder was the main or the only method for the state to acquire food. The destruction caused by the raids in terms of lost lives and property was incalculable. Whole communities were destroyed, carried off into slavery or exterminated. The forces found in the area were the regular army (the jihadiya) who were largely recruited from the Danagala volunteers (former slave traders), the militias known as (*hutteriya*) and local auxiliaries (the *tarjama*, sg. *turjuman*) 'interpreters' or the Turjama were a group of translators that sprang up between the stations and the Bari that acted as middlemen. Each of these armed groups had large units including large households of up to 95 persons per officer. The presence of such a large force exerted a very heavy burden on the surrounding population.[64] The pressure on the populations was such that barely two years after the establishing of a station at Kari and Muggi in 1878, 'all cattle, grain and sesame had disappeared from the area as a result of the frequent raids'.

> "This is the consequence of the system of plunder and robbery that is shamelessly carried out under the name of the official provisioning. If no prompt and energetic measures are taken, the Government will lack the basis to maintain itself within a period of two years."[65]

At first, Gordon got on a lot better with the Bari than with his predecessor, Baker. But, his obsession to extend Khedivial suzerainty to Bunyoro and Buganda kingdoms in Uganda soon detracted him. Soon, he became as unpopular as Baker was. He had to leave in 1876 without having accomplished much in either stopping the slave or developing the Bari. Emin Pasha, in turn, replaced Gordon in 1881.

Emin Pasha (1881–1887)

Emin intensified *ghawe* and ran an extensive network based on personal loyalty and patronage with the local chiefs. He was concerned about the future of his project:

> "If my eventual successor does not interact with the local chiefs the way I do, he will have a very difficult time, since all the chief feel personal loyalty to me because I am generous to them and I take care of them from my own pocket at times when the Government has no money."[66]

To buy loyalty, Emin gave cotton cloth, glass beads, copperware and alcohol to the chiefs. The chiefs, in turn, used these goods to maintain the loyalty of their followers and to reward them for services rendered to both the government and the traders.

Most of the goods came from Khartoum via steamers. These continued to flow until 1878, when the number of steamers coming from Khartoum began to dwindle due to the activities of the sudd. With the reduction on the number of steamers coming to the south bringing more goods, the number of goods available to Emin to buy loyalty from the chiefs also dwindled. By March 1883, a large number of Bari continued to wait for the cargo while others relied on their guns—many of which became available after the partial disbandment of the Egyptian army—to get what they wanted.

The combined Bariland forces opposed to foreign presence under Bepo-lo-Nyiggilo continued to attack government stations and chiefs who had remained loyal to the government. The Fajulu, Nyangwara and the Dinka from Tonj joined in these attacks. The sustained onslaughts on government forces carried out by the people of Ilibari on the road between Rejaf and Lado, and the rebellion of the Rejaf garrison against Emin forced Emin to withdraw his troops finally from Lado in 1887. One year later, in October 1888, the Ansar replaced the Egyptian occupation forces.

Meanwhile, Bepo took full advantage of the siege of Rejaf garrison to settle accounts with the people of Lako-lo-Rondyang, his former friend and rival of his ally and brother in-law, Loro-lo-Lako. Bepo blamed the death of his friend Loro-lo-Lako on the hands of Emin Pasha on Lako-lo-Rondyang and sought to get revenge.

After his defeat at the battle of Rejaf, Emin prepared to withdraw to Wadelay. Many of the troops and the *turjama,* especially those recruited from among the Bari, chose to remain put. Many of them joined the Ansar and wore the jibba. Others remained independent as hired guns and allied themselves to Bari chiefs. Simonse (1992:101) notes that 'in this situation of insecurity the capacity to offer military protection and the distribution of booty became the decisive source of power. A new class of chiefs depending on the gun came to dominate the Bari scene.'[67]

When the Ansar became the dominant power in Bariland, they like their predecessors, relied very heavily on *ghazwe*. They plundered the Bari countryside so thoroughly that they soon turned the general population against them. The main source of resistance against them was the former members of the jihaddiya allied to Bari chiefs and adherents to the 'steamer cult'.

While in northern Bari the centre of resistance against the new invaders, the Ansars, revolved around Gondokoro and Bilinyang, in the south, it was at Barajak at the time when Emin's army withdrew from Kari and Muggi. The new leader of the resistance was a woman, a prophet called Zeinab Kiden, a Fejulu by birth. The forces of Kiden and the Ansar clashed in Kelang in 1890 when the latter attempted to occupy the stations at Kiri and Muggi. In the course of the attack, the former *jihaddiya* who had joined the Ansar deserted en masse, to join the forces of Kiden. The Ansars were decisively defeated and put to flight. By the end of 1891, the Ansar under Commander Umar Salih were forced to withdraw further north to Bor, with only seventy men left, from a contingent of nearly 1500 men. He waited for reinforcement at Bor. Two years later, the Ansar mounted a counter-offensive against the forces of Kiden. This time, they were able to overcome the forces of Kiden and take her prisoner. She was later executed at Rejaf by hanging. The return of the Ansar to Rejaf coincided with the attack on Rejaf by the forces of the Congo Free State, the *tukutuku*.

The Lado Enclave (1897–1907)

With the defeat of Kiden, a number of Bari chiefs who had joined her in the resistance against the Ansars renewed their allegiance to the Mahdists.[68] The Mahdists occupied Bariland for a further four years. However, another occupying force was on the prowl—the forces of King Leopold of Belgium, who were scheming to annex Rejaf to their Empire.

The Ansar did not like the presence of another occupying power in the territory they occupied and prepared to attack them. The Bari did not like the Ansars either, who they blamed for much of the destruction in their land. They sided with the Belgians against Ansars. At their head was Fadl Mualaa jahiddiya who had deserted from Amin's army and had refused to follow him when he was withdrawing southwards to Uganda.

On February 17, 1897, the armies of the Congo Free State and their Bari allies and the Ansars led by Arabi Dafaallah clashed at the battle of Rejaf. In the ensuing battle, the Ansars were completely routed and put to flight. With the defeat of the Ansars, Belgium assumed the administration of that part, west of the Nile, known as the Lado Enclave until 1907.

To the East of the Nile, there was no other foreign force present. Various warlords filled this power vacuum: the *huttoriya*, the *turjama*, the *jihadiya* and deserters from Emin's army. The most important of the warlords was Mödi Adum. Mödi Adum was from Ilibari/Gondokoro and member of the Nyori clan and had worked as a *turjuman* in the days of Emin Pasha. With the fall of the Turco-Egyptian state, he and many others like him switched sides and joined the victorious invading *jihadiya* army. He was at the rank of *emir* when the Mahdist state collapsed in Bariland.

At the battle of Bedden, Mödi together with a force of 1500 strong, mainly Equatorians, 'clad in the *jibba* (Ansar's dress), defected from the *jihadiya* and left Rejaf to seek refuge with Lualla, the chief of Lokiliri, himself a former Mahdist ally'.[69] Mödi Adum became a mercenary who rendered his services to whoever wanted it.

After half a century of internecine war and thorough plundering by a series of vicious bringers and the so-called 'government men', the Bari countryside lay in utter ruin by 1898. Nearly all the formerly populous villages lay destroyed and large number of men and women either killed or carried off into slavery. Lt. Col. Martyr (1899) would give a very grim report of the situation when he came to assume authority of the area on behalf of the Uganda government. 'The number of Bari living between the Uma River and Rejaf, the area characterized by Baker as 'immensely populous' are no more than one thousand'.[70] He observed that:

> "The warlike and troublesome Bari tribe, with whom Baker had so much trouble, are extinct, having been either murdered or taken off as slaves by the Dervishes [Ansars]. Formerly the country must have been thickly populated, for the remains of old villages are very numerous."[71]

The destruction of the Bari was so total that Martyr even proposed that the Lotuko and the Lokoya be resettled in the area that was originally occupied by the Bari. Added to the century of what would now qualify as genocide was the outbreak of small pox and rinderpest epidemics of 1894.[72] Those Bari who survived took refuge in the Lafon and Lulubö hills east of the Nile and in Ma'di and Acholi country.[73]

Balkanization of the Bari: (1898–1906)

As if it were not enough, while Leopold was scheming to annex Equatoria, another power, France was also having similar designs and was on the move. By 1895 Victor Liotard, Govenor General of Upper Ubangi, had established an advanced post on the Sué river in the village of a Zande chief called Tembura and prepared for an advance to the Nile. A force dispatched by Dafaallla Arabi at the end of the year to join the Shakka garrison crossed ahead of the French but were totally destroyed near Tonj in January 1896 by the Nuer who had just joined the war for the first time. 'Provided that they avoided a clash with the Nuer and the Dinka the French now had their path open'(Henderson 1965).

A steamer was put together at Meshra el Rek and Colonel Marchand, who arrived in Tembura's village in July 1896, made his way successfully through the swamps to reach Fashoda exactly a year later. He was still waiting in September when Kicthener arrived in a gunboat, Dal, to claim the country for the Khedive. In March 1899, the French agreed to abandon the southern Sudan and evacuate Fashoda.

Meanwhile, the armies of the Congo Free State and the Ansar under Arabi Dafaallah met in battle south of Rejaf at Beden in 1897 where the Ansars were completely defeated. Arabi withdrew north to Bor where he was once again obliged to retreat in November on the approach of a combined Congolese-British force from the south. With the Mahdists defeated and on the run, King Leopold of Belgium revived his old claim to the whole of Bahr el Ghazal. To appease him, the British had to buy him off with life tenure of the area that was subsequently named 'Lado Enclave'. The Lado

Enclave was the piece of land between the Nile and the 30th meridian south of Latitude 5° 30´. On the east bank of the Nile the boundary between the Sudan and Uganda was vaguely left at 5° N. With Leopold's acquisition of that area, the Bari found themselves effectively divided between three rivalling colonial spheres: (a) the Belgians administered Lado Enclave on the west bank, (b) the Anglo-Egyptian Condominium on the east bank north of the 5th parallel and (c) the administration of the Uganda Protectorate south of it.

The Bariland of 1898 was a divided, chaotic and dangerous place to live in. It was hell on earth. It was a land ruled by feuding chiefs and warlords. "The policy of all three colonial governments was to rely on whatever strongmen were available, regardless of their antecedents".[74] When the Uganda authorities took over the administration of the area, there was general chaos and confusion. To contain the situation, participation in governance of the people in the area was based on comparative power-might. Warlords were made chiefs in place of the weakened traditional rulers. Of necessity, therefore, the country was divided into administrative districts of a size proportionate to the apparent power of the existing chiefs. Thus abler chiefs were put over their less able neighbours. 'As the axiom that power collects power, and might is right, is sound law with these people, the natives soon realised the equity of the present arrangement" (Haddon 1911:471).

Most of the strongmen on the Uganda - administered side were nearly all sons of allies of either the former Turco-Egyptians state, or the *Jihadiya*, and what Simonse (1992:105) termed, "the cargo chiefs". For example, *Kwajok,* the son of *Loro-lo-Lako* who was such a thorn on Baker's side, became the chief of Gondokoro and Bilinyang while at Tokiman/Rejaf, Morbe Bureng, the descendant of Lako-lo-Rondyang "Abu Kuka", became chief.

New on the scene, however, was Mödi Adum, who was not originally the son of a chief. We recall that Mödi was of the Bari who had taken up employment as a soldier first, with the Egyptian government and then Jaddiya but refused to withdraw southwards with Amin Pasha when Egyptian authority in Equatoria collapsed. Like the rest of the deserters, he earned his livelihood as a mercenary. He was the strongman the Uganda administration found in the area and made the chief of Pager. At Logo, Kirba Lokole who had been sent to Omdurman *(Buga)* to meet the Khalifa assumed power after his father. At Tombur, the chief was *Könyi-lo-Jalinga*. *Könyi*, with his able general *Kulang,* had put up a stiff resistance against the Mahdists and successfully repulsed their onslaught on the people of Tombur.

Each of these chiefs was allowed to retain their armies and was responsible for their own defence, especially in the eventuality of attacks by the Lokoya or the Lulubö. The colonial administration limited its role to mere arbitration of conflicts and offering military support in case of serious threat.

Due to devastation of the country, originally habitable areas became infested with tse-tse flies. Accordingly, the remaining villages were relocated away from the infested areas to live along the new road in order to protect the population from the ravages of the tse-tse fly, which had become a menace in these areas.

Wars of succession

The imposition of warlords as new chiefs on the people was not well received by the people, most especially by the children of the traditional rain chiefs or the land chiefs. Predictably, these groups became a threat to the new established order especially at Sindiru. Thus, the problem faced by the colonial administration was in defining the new chiefs' rights in relation to the older rights of the Rainmakers. This conflict resulted in tension and wars of succession.

At Sindiru, there were three main factions competing for succession. One faction was led by *Wani Yemba 'dija*, the son of *Pitya-Yeng-ko-Piong*. The second was championed by *Leju-lo-Lugör*, the senior son of the first wife of Lugör. And the third was under the leadership of Jada and Wani, sons of Lugör's second wife of *Lugör-Möjukulu,* the sister of Lualla, the chief of Lokoya of Lokiliri.[75] To fight their wars of succession, the rain princes had to rely on their alliances with the warlords who in fact turned out to be the decisive factor in the struggle.

In the struggle for power that ensued, the first fight was between Wani-Yemba-'dija supported by the warlord and government chief, Kirba-lo-Lokole against Lualla, supported by Mödi Adum, who was also Lualla's in-law. Pitya-lo-Loyongo led the joint forces of Mödi Adum's men and the *monyomiji of Likiliri* against the forces of Wani-Yemba-'dija and Kirba Lokole. Unfortunately, Pitya Loyongo was killed by Kirba. Mödi Adum took offence and in a second round of fighting, he took revenge. He kidnapped Wani-Yemba-'dija and killed him. After the death of Wani, Mödi Adum chose and supported the candidacy of Leju-lo-ugör.

With the exception of Sindiru, there does not seem to have been wars of succession between the government chiefs and the rain chiefs further north in Bariland. At Bilinyang, the candidacy of Bambu, the grandson of Subek, went unchallenged. Of the children of the former rain chiefs, none became government chief. All of them became sub chiefs, or *mukungus,* under the tutelage of the warlord or government chiefs. For example, Leju-lo-Lugör became a *mukungu,* of Kirba at Logo; Bambu, the grandson of Subek, the former rain chief of Bilinyang became the sub chief of Kwajok, of Gondokoro. For the most part, the position of rain chiefs in Bari society became of ritual significance only.

The Rain chiefs did not give up the fight easily. As early as 1902, there were several attempts at come back by the children of the former rain chiefs. At Pager, for example, there was a serious uprising against the chieftainship of the strongman, Mödi Adum. The revolt was led by a cohort of disgruntled ex-soldiers cum-leaders, such as Kajikir, a descendant of Pönyili Rainmakers of Muggi-Remonyo, and the prophetess Mursillah. Tombe Musa, the son of Mödi Adum, crushed the rebellion. A further challenge to Mödi Adum's chieftainship came from Gumbiri who claimed to be the brother of the rain chief of Kellang. Gumbiri mobilized the people of Kellang, Nyongkir, Gwo'diang, and Muggi, and took their grievances to the Ugandan authorities. Their claim to the chieftainship was recognized and he was made a *mukungu* under Tombe Musa and finally a chief in his own right. However, according to Haddon (1909), Gumbiri was merely the *kölipönit* 'boy' of the Rain chief of Kellang.

Government chiefs

In 1909, Leopold, the Belgian king, died. His death made it possible to readjust the borders and to reunite the Bari once more and in 1913, the Bari were reunited under one colonial administration-the Anglo-Egyptian Condominium. However, until 1906, the Bari formed part of Upper Nile Province, with a post at Mongolla. In the same year, Mongolla was upgraded from a district to a province once again. In 1930 the provincial headquarters was relocated from Mongolla to Juba and the province lost its separate identity.

By the 1930s, peace had returned to Bariland. However, the effects of devastation caused by years of practically continuous spoliation in the frenzied search for slaves, cattle and ivory had left indelible marks on the people and the country. According to L.F. Nalder (19:322),

> "The population had decreased; fly areas had increased; the cultivation of grain is in parts little more than sufficient for the season's needs, while the almost legendary tusks of the old hunters can be found no more."

Gone were the teeming herds of cattle that were the pride of the elephant hunters, bringing in its wake far reaching socio-economic, cultural and political changes.

10

Socio-Political Change

This chapter, we give a bird's view assessment of the social, cultural, economic, political and religious changes that took place in Bari society after the devastating foreign invasions ended.

By all accounts, the Bariland of the early twentieth century that was left after nearly a century of unbridled plunder and rape was a far cry from the robust, vibrant, wealthy and proud nation of the fifteenth century witnessed by foreign visitors. The previously numerous, assertive, tall and fearless population that reminded Werne (1848:288) of 'Roman aristocrats and Egyptian murals that might constitute "a protoplasm of the black race" that once teemed the country, had been reduced to pockets of traumatized, timorous and taciturn people.[76] What were left were desolate remnants of isolated hamlets, made of sickly, cantankerous and impoverished old men and women and a mob of ill-tempered, and brawly young men, prone to unmitigated violence.[77] Simonse (1992:80) dubbed this epoch, 'the Passing of the glamour'. Gone too were the huge herds of cattle that were the pride of the Bari and the envy of neigbours as well as foreigners alike. The abundant wildlife that once roamed the Bari countryside were also destroyed. The destruction was so total that Martyr (1899), would remark that 'the warlike and troublesome Bari with whom Baker had some much trouble are extinct...'[78]

Christianity and Islam in Bariland

Islam

The introduction of foreign religions to Africa be it Islam or Christianity have left deep scares in the African pysche. In Africa, foreign oppression proceeded hand in hand with the Bible and the

Koran. This was also the case in Bariland. What was common to the Arab slave traders and Western missionaries was their attitude towards the African. They shared a common loathing for African values, cultures, traditions and religions. The African was regarded as 'a savage', 'a cursed son of Ham' and big children' that needed to be educated and civilized (Baur 1994:420). They were *tabula rasas*, empty vessels devoid of religious sentiment and culture that should be easily replaced or filled in with Western or Islamic values, traditions and religions. It was the burden of the Whiteman or Arab to provide that service for which the African should be internally grateful.

Although Islam was introduced to the Sudan sometime in the early seventeenth century by itinerant Arab merchants, the 'jalaba', from across the Red Sea, fukaha, 'holy men' and adventurers, it was inadvertently introduced in the southern Sudan in the early part of the 20th century by Arab slave traders and by the Egyptian government during the Turco-Egyptian rule in the Sudan in 1821. The spread of Islam was accidental because, until recently, it was not the intention of the Arab slave traders to convert the Negroes, whom they consider as infidels, into Islam because it would work directly against their interests, for Islam expressly prohibits one Moslem from mistreating, let alone enslaving, another fellow Muslim. Morally then, it would have made their slaving activities extremely difficult, if not impossible. The fact that the Arabs considered the Negroes soulless unbelievers, almost nonhumans enabled them to do extremely cruel things to them. However, those who converted to Islam were promptly released and recruited into the bazingir, or slave army. The Moslems did not open any mosques or kalwas in Bariland. Many of the Bari who converted to Islam were those who had been recruited into the foreign armies, especially, the Mahdiya and Turco-Egyptian army. The depredation done by the Arab Islamic slave traders to the Bari did not endear them to their way of life and their religion.

The Mahdi's uprising of 1884 that brought to an end the hated Turco-Egyptain rule in the Sudan brought much needed relief from exorbitant and extortionist taxes but it did not bring commensurate reprieve to the ravaged part of the southern Sudan, although southerners also joined in the liberation of the Sudan from the hated Turks and the Egyptians. Instead, the Mahdist went out of their way to intensify slaving activities in the south with even greater zeal causing more widespread destruction in the region. With pressure mounting from the British public to end the slave trade and to avenge the death of General Gordon, Britain was forced to invade the Sudan and overthrow the Islamic regime in 1898. As pointed out in Nyombe (1997:99–130), the colonial government immediately put in place very restrictive measures, virtually separating the north from the south.

The Arabic language, Islam and other Moslems practices were proscribed in the south. Moslem names and dressing code were disallowed in the south. Christian sects, divided into spheres of influence, were allowed sway in the south. The missionaries opened schools, dispensaries and maternity wards in the south. From 1900 to 1946, the south and north were ruled as two separate countries, with visas required to travel from one part of the country to the other as per the stipulations of the Closed District Ordinances of 1922 and 1936. This policy, termed the 'Southern Policy' was kept in place until 1946 when it was abruptly changed in 1947 uniting the two halves of the Sudan once more, but under very controversial circumstances.[79]

Christianity

Christianity first came to Bariland in the 1850s, most of the missionaries being of Austrian extraction.[81] Their mission was not a success. Many died. The few that remained did not make serious impact on the society. Some, such a Fr. Vaudey who also doubled as the consul for Sardinia, participated in the slave trade.

Like the Arabs before them, the missionaries shared a common disdain of the African and the Bari. The African was a heathen, and unbeliever who worshipped idols. He was an animist. He lived in sin and he must be saved from himself. He must be shown the right way.

Figure 7: *View Northwards from Juba, Jebel Lado in the distance (The Bari)*

It was, therefore, the duty of civilized nations to win these benighted creatures to God and civilization. Kaufmann, one of the Austrian missionaries at Gondokoro, writes that 'except for a vague knowledge of a Creator and the domestic cult of the black viper, the only religion among the Bari is that of the belly'. And he said this at the time when the Bari were in the middle of a terrible famine that lasted five years, from 1855 to 1860, that nearly wiped out the Bari of Bilinyang and Gondokoro where the drought appears to have been localized. While the food stores of the Austrian mission at Gondokoro were full to bursting with grain and maize, most probably stolen from the neighbouring villages, during the height of the famine, the mission could not provide even a piece of grain to the starving Africans. Instead, they locked their gates and kept the starving people out. It was in this situation that the Bari attacked, looted and burnt down the mission. As the saying goes, 'a hungry man is an angry man.' Any other people would have done the same without having to believe in 'the religion of the belly'.

Generally, the missionaries at Gondokoro were under the mistaken impression that the Bari had no religion and that they were, in fact, irreligious, almost agnostic and nihilists. The Bari were, "neither religious nor superstitious, and not an idolator either but an absolutely earthly human being who only strives for transitory gods: women, cattle and glass-beads' (Hansal, 1876:302). The missionaries (Hansal 1876) and (Kirchner, 1874) dismissed the Bari *ŋun* (God) as essentially evil:

> They could not be convinced that God whom they had a vague idea was good. To the contrary, they maintained that He was evil (aloron), because He sends death, and is responsible for the sun, which burns all their crops' (Morlang, 1874:112).

Kirchner thought that the Bari believed more in their Rainmakers than in a supernatural God to whom they perform a great deal of sacrifice to placate him to protect them from all sorts of ills. He complains that the Bari 'talk a great deal about the miracles wrought by King Nyiggilo, but have no more than a most obscure notion of 'Ngun'. He complained that whenever he inquired about Nyiggilo, one miracle was related to him after another. He was told that Nyiggilo made the sun; that he also made it rain and so on. Overall, he concluded that the Bari did not have any knowledge of something called God nor did they know of His name. Only a few people near the river knew of an evil *Ngun* who killed people and animals'. In utter disdain, Baker contemptuously dismissed the Bari, a people he had never liked at all and helped destroy as:

> "These savages, utterly devoid of belief in a Deity, and without a vestige of superstition, believed most devotedly that the general affairs of life and the control of the elements were in the hands of their old chief' (Baker, 1876, vol. 1:322) also Simeon (1992:87).

With these feelings, it is little wonder that the Catholic mission among the Bari, in Gondokoro, did not succeed.

Even when schools were opened in Bariland later on in the mid 1930s, very few Bari children attended these schools. Chiefs and well to do Bari did not send their children to school because they did not trust the missions. Schooling was limited to the learning of English, reading, writing and some arithmetic. The greater part of the time was dedicated to catechism, learning to recite the rosary and manual work, mostly doing chores for the missions. Pupils were made to stay for inordinately long periods at the missions, sometimes for as long as four years before they were baptized. The four years or so were necessary in order to expunge pagan and barbaric practices from the pupils. They were not to participate in tribal rituals of any kind such as ancestor worship; tribal dances; initiation rites; death funerals and so on. Indulging in any such activity was to commit sin, which must be duly confessed to every Sunday.

The colonial government did not fund education in the south.[8] Education was left in the hands of the under-resourced missions. They were required to teach only the three basic skills of reading, writing and Arithmetic (in the vernacular) and English. English was the official working language in the southern Sudan. Colonial administrators were instructed to speak to the natives in English or their local languages which they were expressly ordered to learn. They were never to talk to the locals in Arabic at any cost. It was believed that too much education was not good for the African because it would adulterate his pristine African character, alienate him from his people and make him feel like a Whiteman. Consequently, it was not until 1948 that the only secondary school for boys was opened in Rumbek.

The repeal of the Closed District Act in 1946 once again linked the south to the north albeit ill prepared for the change. It once opened the floodgate for Arab migrants and traders. A huge exodus of Arab migrants and merchants began to move south. With the change, Arabic once again displaced English in many social and official contexts. Koranic schools and mosques were opened all over the south. The Southerners resented this.

In 1955, the south rebelled. In January 1, 1956, the Sudan got its independence from Britain in spite of the mutiny in the south. From 1956 to 1972, the northern government to whom the colonialist left the rein of power went on a revenge streak. The Southern Policy, put in place by the colonial administration from 1900 to 1946, had to be reversed at any cost because it was 'separatist', anti-north, and anti-Moslem. In accordance with the new policy, all missionary and colonial institutions and structures were brought under the control of the government. Private schools, hospitals and seminaries were either closed down or nationalized. The mission schools were regarded as hotbeds for breeding anti-Islamic and anti-Arab sentiments among southern Sudanese. The teaching of English was abolished and Arabic became the language of instruction. The village school system that was run in the local languages for the first two to three years in the child's mother tongue were abolished. The local languages no longer had any role in education or in any domain.

The insensitivity inherent in the implementation of the new policy by the new Arab dominated government pushed the south into rebellion. Now, since Bariland (Juba) was once again still the seat of government, it was thrown into turmoil with the out break of the war between the north and the south.

Bariland was again in the thick of the war that broke out in 1955 and continued up until 1972 when it was resolved in an agreement known as the Addis Abba Agreement which was brokered in Addis Abba, Ethiopia. The same cycle of violence was repeated in the area. Many Baris lost their lives in the Anya-nya which lasted for 17 years (1955–1972); many more went into exile. They lost the remaining cattle that they had started to restock.

Socio-political change

The radical change in the demography of the Bari had an immediate impact on the political and social organization of the Bari people. Spagnolo (1933:231) points out that in terms of political authority, the *monyekak* (chief of the land) was the ultimate power on the land and his origin predated that of the *matat-lo-pioŋ* (The Rain chief). He was the one that held counsel in Bari land. The appearance of the Rain Chief and the attendant competition for authority that ensued, between the aboriginal *monenyekak* and the Rain chief, caused a great deal of tension, and at times, very violent civil strife in Bari society.

Politically then, one of the main problems faced by the various administrations was to resolve the contradiction arising from the existence of two centres of power and definition of rights between the traditional Rain-chiefs and the warlords. Fifty years after the death of Nyiggilo, the position of the Bari Rain chief has been reduced from one that had considerable political, judicial, and economic power to a purely ritual role.

As we have seen, the colonial administrations gave real political power to the warlords, who became known as *kimaki ti gela* (government chiefs). After the reunification, the colonial administration attempted to accommodate the Rain-chiefs. These were promoted to be government chiefs on equal footing with the warlord/chiefs. Pitya Lugör was one of the few sons of the Rain-chiefs who made a successful come back at Sindiru. His long reign from 1912 to 1949 revived the glamour and grandeur of the Rain chief. Lugör reinstated the solemn procession of traversing Bariland once a year. 'He traveled along the east bank and then along the west bank, making rain, healing the barren, expelling evil from the Bari communities and accumulating big herds of cattle received in tribute' (Seligman, 1934).

The role of settling disputes between chiefs had been, in the past, taken over by the colonial administration. Until his death in 1949, Pitya Lugör remained the only single symbol of Bari unity and identity.

A famous story is told about a contest between Lugör and Captain Cooke, the District Commissioner of Juba from 1926 to 1946. Cooke had built a potoon bridge across the River Nile in 1946 to enable allied troops on their way from Leopoldville to the battlefields in North Africa to cross the river. Captain Cooke showed the bridge to Lugör and boasted of his superior ability to control water. Pitya Lugör is said to have challenged Cooke and told him he would make it rain so hard that his bridge would be swept away in the resulting torrent in a matter of days.

Whether it was Pitya's power, or a natural coincidence, it did indeed rain and Captain Cooke's potoon bridge was swept away in the ensuing deluge as Pity Lugör had predicted. The incident reinforced Lugör's standing among the Bari and is still being talked of even today.

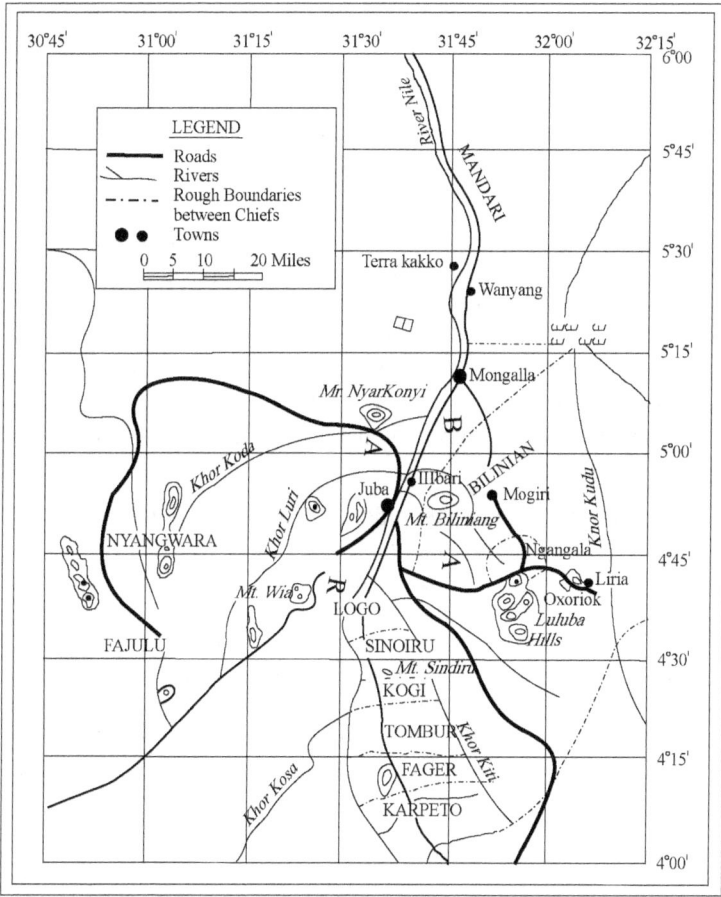

Figure 8: *Sketch Map of the Central District: Mongolla Province*

Sources: (Sudan Notes and Records; Madiya Files, 1732:48)

Another important change that took place was in the social stratification of Bari society. First, the stark social distinction that existed between the social classes among the Bari had all but vanished. The first to be destroyed was the age-set system. This was a social organization known *as ber* into which young men and young women were organized – similar to the Maasai moran. Most of the able bodied, the young men and women having been either carried off by the slavers or perished in the course of the resistance, this institution became useless. Gone were also the initiation rites of passage of becoming of age.

In the past, the Bari were a rigidly stratified society made up of freemen, serfs and slaves. These classes were the *Lui* or freemen, the *Tomonok* or artisans, and the *'Dupi* or serfs. *Tomonok were of two types*: *Tomonok ti Yukit* or the artisans of the forge and the *Yari* or hunters. The *Yari* were further organized into two specialized groups; namely: the hunters of big game such as elephants, buffaloes and so on, known as the *Ligo* and *Tomonok ti kare* or river hunters.

The *tomonok* constituted the middle tier of Bari social stratification. The first group among the *tomonok,* the *Yari,* hunted for the freemen. They lived apart from the Lui and away from the Nile in the open forest. They neither cultivated nor owned cattle. They lived on wild fruits, honey, termites (*konga*), *kite* or tamarind and mushrooms. They paid tribute of meat, honey, elephant tusks, and *kite lisi* (sweet tamarind) to their chief. When they wished to marry, they would come to their chief and beg him to assist them by giving a bull and a cow-calf *(tagwok)* which was the customary bride price of the servile classes.

Like the *Yari,* the *tomonok ti yukit* and *tomonok ti kare* also lived apart from the freemen, the *Lui*. They also lived apart from each other in separate villages according to their respective professions. Their huts were smaller than those of the freemen.

As for the blacksmith, his job was to make implements such as pottery, bowls, and arrows, hoes, spears, large hippopotamus harpoons *(koro)*, knives, trinkets and other tools required by the freemen. The second group is largely fishermen. They lived along the Nile and hunted for hippos, crocodiles, fish and other marine animals. Like the *yari*, they paid tribute in the form of ten to fifteen hoes to the chief. Occasionally, they worked as domestic servants. They rarely intermarried with the freemen.

The lowest class in the Bari social order was the *'dupi* or *'dupi kaderak* (cooks). The *'dupi* were physically distinct from the Lui. They tended to be short, hairy, of reddish tinge and aged a lot faster than the average freemen (Whitehead 1933:30). Their sole function was to cook for the freemen especially during social occasions. When a chief or wealthy nobleman died, he was often buried with his *'dupet*.

Against this background of specialized occupational classes, stood the *Lui,* or freemen. Now, the freemen represented the superior, aristocratic cattle-owning element of the Bari society. The ownership of cattle, the 'possession of the principal posts of the state and general sense of superiority, mark them off from the servile classes' (Whitehead 1933). Not all freemen had cattle but even poor freemen did not run the risk of becoming serfs.

The other change that occurred was the death of the Kurumi, the symbol of cattle wealth and pastoral life. As we have already seen, in the past, the kurumi was the centre of acculturation of the young. That was where they spent most of their teenage and some of their adolescence lives. The demise of the kurumi was also the destruction of what was associated with that institution. It signaled not only the loss of the means of livelihood, but the loss of a whole way of life of a people.

Socio-economic change

The introduction of cash economy helped to free both the lower classes: the *yari* and the *tomonok*. The *yari* were the most fortunate in that regard. The foreigners who came to Bari country needed ivory and *yari*, being elephant hunters, were the only ones who could provide that commodity. They became very wealthy. Some Yari became wealthier even than freeman. They could now own cattle and could therefore afford to marry into the upper families, a thing unheard of in the past. Though they retained their social standing, some lui also turned to elephant hunting for ivory in order to get cash, thereby blurring the dividing line between the social classes.

The blacksmiths too began to earn money and prosper. In the old days, hoes, trinkets and so on were purchased with milk. With nearly all the cattle gone, milk became scarce, instead *dura* (some sort of grain) and honey was given in exchange. Instead of paying for cattle in bride price as they used to, the Bari now gave goats and hoes in bride price. While in the old days cattle were owned by prominent freemen, now all classes *tomonok,* slave and freemen were now owned cattle. Because of this, even the *'dupi* could now marry from the freemen.

The off-shot of all this is that the servile classes became independent in their marriage arrangements and other material needs. They were now able to marry independently from their chiefs and therefore owed them nothing. This fact nullified the chief's claim on services and unquestioned loyalty. The chief's only claim on them was now based only on traditional right. The *'dupi*, because they had very little other than their services to offer, were not so lucky. Only a few of them managed to emancipate themselves through hard work. Until recently, the *'dupi* still cooked for the freemen during ceremonies.

In summary, the Bari society of the fifteenth century and the Bari society of the nineteenth or early twentieth centuries are two different societies. The loss of the basic means of livelihood-cattle and destruction of the population led to a radically changed social structure, social relations and cultural practices among the Bari society. The dislocation of the pastoral way of life of the Bari led to the adoption of a new way of life. From pastoralists, their way of life changed to an agrarian mode of existence. The young men and young women, who were in the past occupied with the cattle, now joined the older men to work in the fields. Today, some Bari communities do not even remember that they once owned cattle, although their songs still revolve around cattle.

End Notes

1. Cf. M. Merker, 1904. Essentially, Marker believed that the Maasai and the Tattog/Datooga were a Semitic race lost in the heartland of Africa and they are to be found in East Africa.
2. Aware of the controversy inherent in the definite of race, the term 'race' here, for the purposes of this discussion is used to loosely refer to ethnicity or community.
3. This does not deny that there was a south-north migration.
4. The Nyepo are actually a part of what are called 'proper' Bari, only they reside on the border between the Bari and the Kuku.
5. These class distinctions do not exist any more, though the Bari are still aware of them. Nobody is allowed to discriminate against anybody based on social origin.
6. This is pretty much like what the Dinka are practising today.
7. Many rich men and chiefs often have many of these hangers-on known as kölipön- it/ök as a mark of respect.
8. See Whitehead, (1962:140–141) and also Spagnolo (1963:303) for details.
9. There is a great deal of difference between the bridewealth being paid at the present and in the past before the Bari lost their cattle to the Turks, Arabs and to Sir Samuel Baker's raids.
10. Cf. Spangolo, L.M. (1933:303).
11. With the cattle gone, this is not being practised today, including the naming of a special bull, although much of Bari personal sons still refer to it.

12. There are also *mamaresi*, or specific words, that a man utters loudly especially when he is in a good mood or in trouble. When uttered, it would immediately be recognized by everybody in the community and they would come to his rescue when necessary.
13. Sir Samuel Baker found that out when he conducted a cattle raid at the village of Bilinyang.
14. These crops are also grown by the other Bari-speakers.
15. Whitehead, (1962:137), claims that the word *sörömöndi* 'hardly sounds like a true Bari word'. It is used by the Mondu and turns as far away as in Nigeria, under the form of *siyara gunda.*
16. The other Bari-speaking tribes, especially the Fajulu and Kakwa use a slightly different naming system, but see Whitehead (1962:135–36)
17. Cf. August Scheilcher, Die Darwinsche Theorie und die Sprachwissenschaft (Berlin, 1863): see also Herman Paul, Prinzipien der Sprachgeschichte, in (Halle 1909).
18. Cf. Greenberg, (1950:143–160) for further arguments in support of this view.
19. Cf. G.W. Murray and M.C.F. Roy (1920).
20. See Murray and Roy (1920:267), in Sudan Notes and Records.
21. J.J. Bachofen (1938:89) "Du Règne de la mèré au patriaarcit, "quote from Diop 1974.
22. Greenberg supported this view, but see footnote 1 in Greenberg (1950:143) Vol. 6. There, he asserts that the term Hamitic 'does not refer to any valid linguistic entity'.
23. See Ehret (1973:3) to see how the comparative linguistic method is used in the reconstruction of unwritten languages using linguistics cognates.
24. There are scholars who are of the opinion that, what are known variously as Cushites, Egyptians, Ethiopians, Axumites, Nubians, Hamites and Sudanese are really nothing but racial designations representing the same people—Nilotes. These terms have the same meaning. They mean

black. These epitaphs were given by foreign invaders who had lived among the blacks.

25. Spangolo (1933:XII) classified Kuku and Nyangwara as originally belonging to the Lokoya sub-tribes, but see his footnote 4 on page XIII.

26. Cf. G.W. Murray, (1920:360). The Nilotic Languages, a Comparative Essay, (Journal, Royal Anthropological Institute, vol. 50, pp. 327–368).

27. The Lotuho remembered these people as the Ongadule or Cangadule, Tongotole by the Lulubo, and Guruguru by the Pari. Amin Pasha, (Tagebcher, vol. 1:215) was told that small people existed in the forests west of the Nile. He believed these people to be the Namnam mentioned by ancient Egyptians.

28. There are a group of people in Eritrea who until recently still call themselves Bari-ya. They say that they had brothers who had left them there and went away. If true, this would independently corroborate and therefore support what is being suggested here.

29. Cf Ehret, 1971.

30. See Hassan (1967?).

31. I understand in both Eritrea and Ethiopia, the term Bari came to be closely associated with slavery. To avoid the social consequences of such unfavorable associations, the group was forced to expunge the offending word from its vocabulary. It is especially more so when the word 'Bari' is said to mean 'slave' in Amharic.

32. This dirge is still being sung in Lotuho today.

33. There are a number of versions to this story. See Simonse (1992:59).

34. Grouping the Fajulu, Nyagwara and Kuku as belonging to the Lokoya subtribe looks very odd indeed. If they were, then they must have been totally assimilated by the Bari to such an extent that they lost their languages. Based on linguistic evidence, no such assimilation seemed to have taken place.

35. Cf Beaton, (1934: 170–172).
36. Classifying the Lulubo together with the Lokoya is odd because the former belongs to the larger Eastern Sudanic group which includes among others, Muru-Madi-lugbara tribes.
37. Actually, thirty-five years would be a little more accurate. In the past before things fall apart after the invasion of Bariland, the Bari used to live long and a person was said to have died young if he or she died at the age of sixty.
38. It is important to note that the assumed chronological dating would change quite considerably if we assumed that 35 years constitutes a generating instead of 20 years as suggested by Beaton.
39. Note that this story conflicts with the myth that the Bari originally came from the east, from around the shores of Lake Rudolf (Lake Turkana). This therefore points to a different possibility that, in fact, the Bari migrated to their present location from the North, rather than from the east.
40. Beaton notes that the real name of Wani Yemba 'Dija (means closed marriage) was Wani lo-Lugör. He was so nicknamed because he had no children despite his many wives.
41. Cf. Lt. Col. Martyr, Report on the Nile District of the Uganda Protectorate', Inclosure 1, in Dispatch 76 from Acting Commissioner Kampala; Uganda National Archives, Foreign Office, Correspondence, East Africa, May 18, 1899.
42. This Lokuryeje must be different from Lokuryeje the 'diviner'.
43. Cf. Whitehead, (1932:).
44. See Beaton (1934: 176).
45. See Beaton (1934:180–181).
46. About 1972, the people from Gondokoro who had followed Mödi to Pager returned to northern Bari and are settled around Gumba area in Juba.
47. See Seligman, pp. 75–478.

Rather, the observed differences may be attributed to normal dialectal variations common in any natural language.

48. Swökir has now disappeared and was probably a little north of Kujönök and east of the stream of Leleba, on the Juba Mongolla road which has also disappeared. The latter because of the lack of maintenance due to the first and present war (1955–to-present).
49. Franz Morlang, "Reisen östlich und Westlich von Gondokoro, 1859," Petermann's Mittheilungen Ergänzungsband, II, 1862–3, p. 116.
50. This story is current among the Bari but a little different. Word had reached Emin Pasha from his local spies that Chief Lako had named his dog 'Emin Bey' after him. Enraged at the news, he paid Lako a visit and enquired about the name of dog. Sensing danger, Lako of course did not say. Drawing his sword, he ordered Lako to call the dog. The dog came running on hearing the name 'Emin Bey'. At this, Emin drew his sword and struck off the head of Chief Lako.
51. Cf. Werne, Nouvelles Annales de Voyage, Vol.3, p11, 1862.
52. Werne, (1848:288, 292).
53. See Nouvelles Annales de Voyage, Vol. 3, p11, 1862. This is probably the "Alloron" of Baker. He was actually known as Loro-lo- ojurön (Loro the foreigner).
54. Nyiggilo is said to have told Brun-Rollet the following: " I leave myself in your hands. I want to know the country that produces the fruits and drinks that you have given me to taste; I want to see how woven fabrics and the other objects in your possession that I admire are manufactured. They prove that your people are superior to us who cannot produce anything of the like. If you give me some of the articles, I will return to my country as a rich and powerful man either with you, if you wish so, or with the people you confide to me to buy ivory (Brun-Rollet 1885:188).
55. Quoted from Simonse (1992:92), but also refer to his footnote 40.
56. See Gray, 1961:131.
57. This is a story often recounted when people talk about what happened during the *Kotoriya* or *Jaddiya* periods (The Turkish and Mahdiya invasions).

58. See Baker Ismailia, pp 108.
59. Cf. Baker S.W. (1871:157) Ismalia, A narrative of the Expedition to Central Africa for the Suppression of the Slave Trade.
60. Cf. Simonse, S. (1992:95).
61. Cf. Moorhead, 1910:81.
62. Moorhead ibid, 157.
63. Cf. Junker, (1889:303).
64. Hassan, 1896, vol. 1:62.
65. Emin Pasha, (Tagebücher, vol. 11:39)
66. Emin Pasha in Central Africa.
67. Simonse, (1992:101).
68. Letter to Arabi Dafa'alla to the Khalifa, 12 Jamada 1311, Central Records Office, Madiya Files, 1/32:48.
69. Report on Nile Province, 1902', Uganda National Achieves, Entebbe, Shuli Correspondence A16–2:52.
70. Lt. Col. Martyr (1899), 'Report on the Nile District of Uganda Protectorate'. Inclosure 1, Office. *Correspondence*, East Africa.
71. Cf. Letter from D.Z. Carré from Dufile, 1/2/1899, Central Records Office, Khartoum. INTEL/5/5/49: 'Uganda Reports', also cited in Smonse (1992:03).
72. Yuzbashi, (1905:227).
73. This would be a second forced refuge. Recall that the Bari were forced to flee to south during the invasion of the Lomukudit in the eighteen century.
74. E.B. Haddon, (1911:471).
75. Recall that Lualla was a nephew of the Bekat of Sindiru.
76. Verne, (1884:295) had this to say about the Bari: 'As with virtus of the Romans, courage is the common denominator of all their virtues, to which all other qualities springing from their pure, uncorrupted, nature are subordinated'.
77. Brun-Rollet (1855:250), Beltrame 1881:302–303) and others noted that Bari men died as result of violence than disease.

78. Lt. Col. Martyr, 'Report on the Nile District of Uganda Protectorate', Inclosure 1, in Despatch 76 from Acting Commissioner Kampala; Uganda National Archives, Foreign Office. Correspondence, East Africa, May 18, 1899.
79. Cf. Nyombe, (199:105). See also the Civil Secretary's secret Despatch No. 89, August, in the Central Archives of the Ministry of the Interior (Sudan Government Document 1945).
80. Cf. Jömbi, C.L. (1989:107–123): Juridic Structure of the Christian Church in the Sudan.
81. Cf. Sanderson, (1962, SNR, XLIII, vol. 43).

Bibliography

Bachofen, J.J. (1938:89), "Du Règne de la mèré au patriaarcit.

Baker, S.W. (1872), "Ismailia". *A Narrative of the Expedition to Central Africa for the Suppression of the Slave Trade.* IndyPulish.Com. Mclean, Virginia.

Battuta, IBN. See H.A.R. Gibb, Ibn Battuta, *Travels in Asia and Africa.* London: 1929. Also: Les Voyages d'Ibn Battuta, translated into French by Défremery and B.R. Sunguinetti. Paris: 1854.

_____. (1962), *"The Albert N'yanza". Great Basin of the Nile and Exploration of the Nile Sources,* Vol. 1. Sidgwick and Jackson. London.

Baur, J. (1994), *200 Years of Christianity in Africa, 'An African Church History',* 2nd (ed). Paulines Publications. Africa.

Beaton, A.C. (1932), 'Bari Studies'. *Sudan Notes and Records, 15/1:62–95.*

_____. (1934), "A Chapter in Bari History", The History of Sindiru, Bilinyang and Mogiri. *Sudan Notes and Records, 17/2:169–200.*

_____. (1936), "The Bari: Clans and Age-Class Systems". *Sudan Notes and Records, 19/1:109–145.*

Beltrame, G. (1881), Il Fiume Bianco e I Dinka. Memorie Verona: G. Givelli.

Brun-Rollet, A. (1855), Le Nil Blanc el Soudan, Etudies sur Afrique Centrale, Moeurs et Coutumes des Sauvages. Paris: Librairie L. Maison.

Buxton, Jean, C. (1963), Chiefs and Strangers, A Study in Political Assimilation among the Mandari. Oxford: Claredon.

Chomsky, N. (1970), *"Current Issues in Linguistic Theory"*. Mounton.

Dimmendaal, G. (1982), Topics in Grammar of Turkana: In, '*Nilo-Saharan Studies*', Lionel Bender (ed), pp 177–207. African Studies Center, Michigan State University.

Diop, C.A. (1974), *The African Origin of Civilization: "Myth or Reality"*. Lawrence Hill and Company Publishers, INC.

Douin, G. (1936–41), *Historie du Règne du Khedive Ismail*, 3 vols. Cairo: La Sociéte Royal Géographie d'Egypte.

Ehret, C. (1971), *Southern Nilotic History: "Linguistic Approaches to the Study of the Past"*. Northwestern University Press. Evanston, Illinois.

Gleason, Henry A., Jr. (1959), "Counting and Calculating for historical reconstruction", AL, 1.2: 22–32. (8).

Graebner, F. (1911), *Methode der Ethnologie, Heidelberg.*

_____. (1963), *The Languages of Africa,* The Hague: Mouton.

Gray, R. (1961), *A History of the Southern Sudan, 1839–1889*: University Press.

Greenberg, J.H. (1957), *Essays in Linguistics*. The University of Chicago Press.

_____. (1955): *Studies in African Linguistics Classification*. New Haven. Compass.

Haddon, E.B. (1911), *"Systems of Chieftaincy among the Bari of Uganda"*, Journal of the African Society, Vol. X, pp 468.

_____. (1991), "Notes on the Ethnography of the Bari." M.A. thesis, University of Cambridge, kept in the Haddon Library, Cambridge.

Hansal, (1876), "Die Bari-Neger", mittheliungen der kais'. Und kön. Geographischen Geselleschaft in Wien, Vol. 19 (Neue Folge), pp 294–307.

Hartmann, R. (1884), *Die Nilländer*. Leipzig: G. Freytag and Prag: F. Tempsky.

Hassan, V. (1893), *Die Wahreheit Über*. Emin Pasha, die Aegyptische Aequatoriaprovinz und den Sudan, 2 Vols. Berlin: Dietrich Reimer.

Herodotus, (1954), "The Histories". Translated by Uabrey De Sélincourt, revised and with an introduction by A.R. Burn. Penguin Books.

Henderson, K.D.D. (1965), *Sudan Republic*. Frederick A. Preager. New York. Washington. Pp (152–202).

Jömbi, C.L. (1988), *Juridic Structure of the Christian Church in the Sudan*, "From the Origin of Christianity in Nubia before and after the Diffusion of Islam". Tipografica "Leberit" via Aurelia 308-Roma.

Khaldun, Ibn. 14th Century Arab Historian.

Lafrague, J. (1845), "Extract of his letter of 1/5/1845, in the 'Voyage au Bahr-el-Abiad (Extract d'une letter de M. le Dr. Perron, date 1/9/1845." Bulletin de la Sociétié de Géographie (Paris), Séries III, 4:159–160.

Lehman, W.P. (1992), "Historical Linguistics", (3ed.) Rutledge.

Lewis, D.L. (1987), *The Race to Fashoda*, "Colonialism and African Resistance". Henry Holt and Company. New York.

Maspero, G. (1917), Historie ancienne des peoples de l'Orient. Paris: Hachette, 1917, 12th ed. Translated as *"The Dawn of Civilization"*. London, 1884.

Meinhof, C. (1917–18), "Sprachestudien im egyptischen Sudan: 29: Kondjara", ZKS 8: 117, 139, 170–195 (4).

Merker, M. (1904), Die Maasai, ethnographische monographie eines ostafrikanishen Semitenvolkes. Reimer.

Mitterrutzner, J.C. (1867), Ddie Sprache der Bari in Central-Africa, Text und Wörterbuch. Brixen.

Morlang, F. (1974), "The Journeys of Franz Morlang East and West of Gondokoro in 1859 Trans. of Morlang (1862/3). In, Toniolo and Hill (eds.), 1974: 109–128.

Moorhead, A. (1910), *The White Nile*. Vintage Books. A Division Random House. New York.

_____. (1862), "Reisen östlich und Westlich von Godokoro, 1859." Petermann's mitteillungen, Erganzungsheift II: 115–124.

Muratori, C. (1938), Grammatica Lotuxo. Verona Missionie Africane.

Murray, G.W. (1920), "The Nilotic Languages: A Comparative Essay", JRAI 50: 327–368. (8).

Murray, G.W. & C.F. Roy (1920), *The Nuba and Bari Languages Compared*, In: The Journal of Royal Anthropological Institute. Vol., l.

Mounteney-Jephson, A.J. (1890), *Amin Pasha and Rebellion at the Equator*. London: Sampson Low, Marston, Searle & Rivington.

Nyombe, B.G.V. (1997), Survival or Extinction: "the fate of the Languages of the Southern Sudan", In *International Journal of the Sociology of Language*; Joshua A. Fishman (ed). Mouton de Gruyter. Berlin. New York.

_____. (1995), *Word Order in Proto-Nilotic*. In Afrikanistische Arbeitspapiere (AAP): editors: Angelika Birkle and Urlike Claudu *et al*. Institut fur Afrikanistik, Universität zu Köln.

Ogot, B. A. (1961), "The Concept jok among the Nilotes." African Studies, 20/2:121–130.

Paul, H. (1909), "Prinzipien der Sprachgeschichte", in (Halle).

Rottland, F. (1982), Southern Nilotic with and Outline of Datooga: In, *'Nilo-Saharan Studies'*, Lionel Bender (ed), pp 177–207. African Studies Center, Michigan State University.

Westermann, (1912), *The Shilluk People*. Berlin.

Whitehead, G.O. (1929), "Social Change among the Bari." *Sudan Notes and Records, 12/1: 91–97.*

_____. (1936), "A Note on Bari History." *Sudan Notes and Records, 19/1:152–157.*

_____. (1950), "Property and Inheritance among the Bari." *Sudan Notes and Records, 31/1:143–147.*

_____. (1953), "Suppress Classes among the Bari, and Bari-speaking Tribes", *Sudan Notes and Records, 34/2:265–280.*

_____. (1962), "Crops and Cattle among the Bari and Bari-speaking Tribes." *Sudan Notes and Records, 43:131–142.*

Glossary of unfamiliar words

Word	Singular	Plural	Meaning
lui	luitöt	lui	Freeman
tomonok	tumunit	tomonok	blacksmith
'dupi	'dupet	'dupi	Slave
mor	mor	moran	Paramount chief
kak	kak	kakan	Land
monyɛ	monyɛ	komonyɛ	father
monyekak	monyekak	komonyekak	Landowner
Matat	matat	kimak	Chief
Pioŋ	pioŋtot	pioŋ	Water
bömön	Bömöntyo/ti	bömön	Freemen associated with rain making
yukit	yukit	yukitön	Forge
yari	yarinit	yari	River hunters/fisherman
lıgo	*ligotot*	lıgo	Big game hunter
Kare	kare	kareya	River
kite	kite	Kiteni'	Tamarind tree
lısı	lısı	lısıjın	Sweet
tagwok	tagwok	Kajak	Calf
koro	koro	koryot	Harpoon
der			To cook
kaderanıt	kaderanıt	kaderak	Cook
rata			To pasture
ratet	ratet	ratesı	Place for pastures
Torobo'	Turu'bunı'	Toro'bo	Property
Ratet na toro'bo	Ratet na toro'bo	Ratesı ti toro'bo	Place for pasturing animals
kurumi	kurumi	kurumiyet	Kraal (cattle camp)

bɛr	bɛrtyo	bɛr	Age mates
mɛjɛ	mɛjɛ	mɛjɛlon	Red ochre
kıtɛŋ	kıtɛŋ	kısuk	Cow
lomore	lomore	Lomoryot/ lomoriot	Private
mat			To drink
matɛ	matɛ	Matɛyat/ matiat	Cow loaned to friend for milking
yema	yema	yemesi	For marriage
Kısuk yɛmesı	Kıtɛŋ yemet	Kısuk yɛmesı	Cow for marriage
nyɛr	nyɛra	nyɛresı	for wedding
kısuk nyɛresı	Kıtɛŋ nyɛret	Kısuk nyɛresı	Bridewealth
dwöt	dwöt	dwonın	Bull
tı	tı	tı	For/possessive
sönö	sönö	sönöyöt	Special bull
mananyɛ	mananyɛ	komananyɛ	Maternal uncle
Lokiko'	Lokiko'	lokikolan	Emissary
mokɛn	mokɛn	mokɛnya	Mother-in-law
torɛ	torɛ	torɛla	Children
Dulö			The act of bending
Dulö na oŋgwora			The act of bending horns
ongwara	uŋgwuri	uŋgwora	Wild beasts
uŋguli	uŋguli	oŋgolat	Sausage fruit
köli	Köli	kölisi	Songs
gotet	gotet	gotesi	Praise
Kölisi gotesi	Köli gotet	Kölisi gotesi	Praise songs
toket	toket	tokesi	Rest place
mole	mole	molesi	Group cultivation
melesen	melesen	meleseno	Fields/farms
ŋun	ŋun	ŋunyön	God
kömu	Kömu	kömuöt	Guests
mulökö	mulökötyo	mulökö	Spirits
miyan	miyanti	miyan	Evil spirits
rubaŋga	rubaŋga	rubanjin	Offerings
daŋ	daŋ	daŋin	

lowe	lowe	loweya	Arrows
gwolo	gwolo	gwulujin	Quiver
'buku	'buku	bukwö	Shield
kala	kele	kala	Tooth

Index

Abu Sa'ud, 113
Acholi, 41
Adum Mödi, 126
Al Aqqad, 113
Anglo-Egyptian Condominium, 131
Ansars, 114, 125
Arab invasion, 89
Arabi Daffaalla, 105
Arabs, 48
Bahr el Gebel, 5
Bahr el Ghazal, 48, 54, 55, 127
Bahr el Ghazal Region, 3
Bari, 41, 43
   agriculture, 11
   Balkanization of, 127
   differences, 68
   height, 68
   in pre-History, 39
   pastoral life, 7
   physical characteristics, 67
   society, 1
   socio-economic organization, 5
   socio-political change, 133, 139
   trade, 107
Bari Dispersal, 90
Bari migration, 51
Bari of northern Bari, 68
Bariland, 4, 72
Bari-Lotuho-Lokoya tribe, 61
Bekat Clan, 75
Bekat Limat, 72
Bekat Manabur, 83
Bepo-lo-Nyiggilo, 102, 124

Berbers, 48
Bhkat Treaty, 51
Bilinyang, 72, 130
Bilinyang/Gondokoro axis, 92
Brun-Rollet, 109
Canaanites, 48
Caucasians, 51
Chief Logunu, 95
Chiefs
   government, 131
Christianity, 135
   in Bariland, 133
Closed District Act, 138
Closed District Ordinances of 1922 and 1936. *See also* Southern policy
Cluster
   Bari, 5
Col. Martyr Lt., 126
Congo Free State, 126
Crimean War, 120
Danagala volunteers, 122
Democratic Republic of the Congo (DRC), xi
Deng, Francis, 4
Dere, 95
Dervishes, 102
Didinga Hills, 70
Dinka, 41, 127
Dongoda, 52
Dungkaliri, 76
dupet, 6
dupi, 6

dura, 11
Eastern Nilotic, 41
Education, 138
Emin, Pasha Muhammed, 101, 103, 123, 124
Equatoria, 5. *See also* Bahr el Gebel
Eritrea, 60
Fadl Mualaa jahiddiya, 125
Fajulu, 44, 69, 124
Forked pole
    and slave trade, 115
Fr. Angelo Vinco, 108
Fr. Vaudey, 109
    and slave trade, 135
Galla incursion, 80
General Gordon, 120
Genetic classification, 42
Gleason classification, 42
Gondokoro, 57, 58, 72, 100
    civil war at, 108
Gordon, 101
Greeks, 48
Hebrews, 48
Herodotus, 67
Huntington, xi
Ilibari, 72, 93, 100
Islam
    in Bariland, 133
Jada Lo Mödi, 83
Jangara, 85
Juan na-Mödi, 83
Juba, 131
Kakwa, 44, 69
Kalenjin, 56
Kaufmann, 136
Keyo, 41
Khartoum, 100
Khedive, 120
King Leopold of Belgium, 125

Kipsigis, 41
Kirba-lo-Lokole, 130
Kuku, 44, 69
Kuwuba, 76, 77
Lado, 91
Lado Enclave, 127
Lado Jangara, 87
Lado-lo-Ide, 101
Lake Albert, 103
Lake Rudolf, xii
Lake Tana, 58
Lake Turkana, 55, 70
Lako, 101
Lako-lo-Rondyang, 121
Land chiefs, 129
Leju-lo-ugör, 130
Liria, 70
Logunu, 97
Lokoro, 77
Lokoya, 52
Lokuryeje, 76, 104
Lomijikotet, 76
Lomukudit, 80
Loro Kimbo, 92
Loro-lo-Lako, 124
Lotuho, 41
Lotuke, xii
Lotuko, 43, 52
Lugbara, 68
Lugör-lo-Pitya, 88
Lulubo, 68
Maasai, 41
Madi, 68
Mahdists, 127
Manabur, 83
Marchand Colonel, 127
Matat Lo Piong, 94
Mödi, 82
Mödi Adum, 92, 128

Mödi Lokuryeje, 81
Mohammed, Ali, 95
Mongalla Province, 61
Mongolla, 131
Mongols, 48
Morsak, 52
Moru, 68
Mount Lotuke, 70
Mountains of the Moon, 96
Mundari, 44, 69
Nandi, 41
Nile Basin, 47
Nilo-Hamites, xii, 56
Nilotes, xii
Nilotic Diaspora, 47
Nilotic history, xiii
Nilotic languages, xii, 40
Nilotic peoples, 41
Non-proto-Western family, 56
Nubian Kingdom, 51
Nuer, 41, 127
Nyangwara, 44, 69, 92
Nyangwaraland, 70
Nyiggilo, 100, 140
Nyori, 76
Nyori Kimak clan, 76
Ogot, Bethwel, 4
Omdurman, 109
Ongamo-Maa, 43
Oxoriok, 66, 84
Phoenicians, 48
Pintong, 76, 77
Pipiri, 76
Pitya, 87
Pitya-lo-Jangara, 87
proto-language, 40
Proto-Nilotes, 71
proto-Nilotic, 40, 41
proto-Western Nilotic, 56

Rain chiefs, 71, 111, 129. *See also* land chiefs
Rainmakers, 137
Rejaf, 125
Romans, 48
Salva Kiir Mayar Dit, General, xiv
Samuel Baker, 101
Sheba, 115
Shilluk, 41
Sindiru, 70, 72, 76
Social stratification, 142
Société de Géographie de Paris, 95
Socio-political change, 133–44
Southern Nilotic Branch. *See also* Kalenjin
Southern Policy, 135
Subek, 100
Subek-lo-Logunu
  and slave trade, 108
Swadesh classification, 42
Teso, 41
Teso-Turkana, 43
The Bari, xi
The Lui, 5
Tombe, 57
Tome Mödi, 82
Tomonok, 6
Toposa, 41
Turco-Egyptian invasion, 71
Turco-Egyptians, 69
Turco-Egyptians state, 128
Turko-Egyptian Sudan, 101
Turks, 90, 114
Victor Liotard, 127
Wani, 91
Wani-Yemba-'dija, 130
Werne, 103
Werne d'Arnand, 95

Western Nilotes, 41
White Nile, 95
Whitehead, 13
Wotoko, 62

Yo'yok, 74
Yure. *See also* Bari
Zeinab Kiden, 125

www.ingramcontent.com/pod-product-compliance
Lightning Source LLC
Chambersburg PA
CBHW070641300426
44111CB00013B/2202